MERLIN
AND
WOMAN

MERLIN
AND
WOMAN

The Second Merlin Conference
London, June 1987

Edited by R. J. Stewart
Illustrated by Miranda Gray

BLANDFORD PRESS
LONDON · NEW YORK · SYDNEY

First published in the UK 1988 by Blandford Press,
an imprint of Cassell plc
Artillery House, Artillery Row, London SW1P 1RT

Distributed in the United States by
Sterling Publishing Co, Inc,
2 Park Avenue, New York, NY 10016

Distributed in Australia by
Capricorn Link (Australia) Pty Ltd
PO Box 665, Lane Cove, NSW 2066

British Library Cataloguing in Publication Data

Merlin Conference; 2nd (1987) :London
  England
  Merlin and women : the Second Merlin
  Conference
  1. Legends. Characters : Merlin
  I. Title   II.Stewart, R.J.
  509'.352

ISBN 0 7137 2015 8

Typeset by Butler & Tanner Ltd, Frome and London

Printed and bound in Great Britain by
Mackays of Chatham PLC, Chatham, Kent

Contents

5

CONTENTS

Part 7 Merlin and the Mother Goddess

LIST OF ILLUSTRATIONS

Acknowledgements

The publication of this book would not have been possible without the efforts of the many contributors and enthusiasts who attended the Second Merlin Conference in 1987. Acknowledgement should be made to the following people, who are listed in alphabetical order: Dolores Ashcroft-Nowicki, Geoffrey Ashe, Lynda Ballinger, John Boorman, Stuart Booth, Eileen Campbell, Denise Coffey, Peter Dickinson, Phillip Dunbar, Heather Formioni, Howard Goorney, Miranda and Richard Gray, Michael Green, Gareth Knight, Alan Lee, John and Caitlín Matthews, Rachel Pollack, Kathleen Raine, Laraine Stewart, Peter Vansittart.

Special acknowledgement is due to Mary Stutters, the Conference Administrator, who contributed at every level to the event. As always the contributors are indebted to the work of earlier writers, poets and bards, particularly Geoffrey of Monmouth and the anonymous Celtic tale tellers from whom the Merlin traditions and other legends were originally drawn.

Acknowledgement must also be made to those little-known and mysterious seers who appear through British history (who are discussed in our various chapters) and to Merlin himself.

R. J. Stewart, 1988

List of Contributors

The contributors are listed here in alphabetical order, which is not their order of appearance in the book nor of the Conference in June 1987.

Dolores Ashcroft-Nowicki has written a number of books on esoteric studies, visualisation, and magical arts. She teaches and lectures worldwide and directs the 'Servants of the Light', a modern school dedicated to imaginative and spiritual development.

Gareth Knight has been instrumental in modern reassessment of Hermetic and Arthurian traditions as a means of altering consciousness. He has written books on Arthurian legend, the Tarot, Qabalah, and Rosicrucian philosophy, and has directed many courses and experiential events based upon these subjects.

Caitlín Matthews is a writer, singer, and harpist. She has published two volumes on Western esoteric tradition: *The Western Way* with John Matthews, and *Mabon and the Mysteries of Britain*, the first of a two-volume study of Welsh legends. She is also co-author of the forthcoming *Aquarian Guide to British Myth and Legend*.

John Matthews specialises in Arthurian studies and the Grail tradition. He has published a number of highly acclaimed books on Grail legends, and is currently preparing an *Arthurian Reader*, a collection of rare articles by Arthurian scholars. His most recent publication is *Warriors of Arthur* with Bob Stewart, which examines the Dark Age Arthur in legend, tales, and history.

Rachel Pollack is a story teller and writer, who specialises in working with tarot. She has published novels and books on tarot and supervised the creation of modern tarot packs.

Kathleen Raine is a poet and scholar and an acknowledged authority on William Blake and his sources in Western esoteric tradition and Neo-Platonism. She has published a number of books on Blake and on Thomas Taylor, the Platonist, and her most recent work, *Yeats the Initiate*, examines the influence of Yeats' magical studies and practices. She is also editor of *Temenos*, a review of the arts of the imagination.

R. J. (Bob) Stewart is a composer and writer. His books include two volumes on the medieval Merlin texts, studies of magical tradition in folklore, the effects of music upon inner development, magical arts, and children's stories. His most recent work is *The Merlin Tarot*, a detailed book on tarot imagery in the *Vita Merlini* with a full-colour deck of cards painted by Miranda Gray. Bob Stewart is editor of both volumes of *The Book of Merlin*, director of the Merlin Conference and author of *The Warriors of Arthur* with John Matthews. He has composed and recorded music and songs for feature films, television, radio, and theatre, plus a number of cassettes and records.

Introduction

This second 'Book of Merlin' places special emphasis upon the relationship between Merlin and Woman, or between Merlin and what is frequently described as 'the feminine principle'. This relationship was the main theme of the Second Merlin Conference held in London in 1987, which set out to destroy the popular delusion that Merlin is a stereotypical wise male elder with no qualities or relationships involving woman, women or the feminine principle.

We are not dealing with an abstract or theoretical quality when we look into Merlin's interaction with Woman; the earliest Merlin texts make it very clear that he related to real live women ... his mother, his sister, his wife, and also to magical or divine feminine images such as the goddess of the land of Britain, the weaver goddess Ariadne and a mysterious woman who tried to bring about his death with poisoned apples (similar in many ways to the fairy queen who rules poisoned fruit in Celtic folk tradition).

Nothing about Merlin, however, is simple or obvious. In the *Vita Merlini* his sister Ganieda, a queen of considerable power,[1] frequently acts as a representative or embodiment of a goddess. She is similar to *Minerva*, a name frequently used by Geoffrey of Monmouth (author but not sole creator of the *Vita*), to describe a Celtic culture goddess found in tradition.

Drawing from traditions, probably retained in story or verse by bardic entertainers and localised story tellers, Geoffrey used classical terms to describe various personae as he assembled and recreated the Merlin tales into his masterpiece. Thus Ganieda seems to devote a great part of her considerable vigour, intelligence and power to steering a rather foolish Merlin towards maturity. The mythic theme is clear: an older sister or culture goddess provides the means whereby a foolish brother or entire race of humankind may grow towards wisdom through experience.

The emphasis is upon the word *experience*, for Ganieda (like the classical Minerva or Athena) does not drop benefits willy-nilly into the hero's lap. She provides, often in a curious and roundabout manner, certain means, adventures and tests, whereby he may grow through experience. She is, like so many feminine images in magical or mystical tradition, a catalyst.

Merlin's wife, Guendoloena, fares less well: she seems at first to be a rather modern stereotype of pseudo-femininity, all beauty, sensuality, overblown emotion, with no strength of will or critical intelligence; but if we scratch this tinsel surface, we find her to be a poorly rationalised representative of the Celtic nature goddess, a being of flowers and spring growth. Like Ganieda, she is both a human and an archetype at once. Many of the personae in the Merlin legends, particularly in Geoffrey's *Vita* tend to represent magical or archetypical beings, often with a seasonal emphasis[1].

The impression gained from the *Vita* is that of a motif in which the aspiring seer or magician must learn to seek beyond sensuality or emotional gratification: in modern psychological terms we might prefer to say that Merlin learns how to relate to women as sisters rather than as sexual toys ... but this, important as it is in a twentieth-century context, is only the most superficial way of interpreting the legend. Examination of Merlin's wife and sister, even in such a brief summary, immediately disposes of the common image of Merlin living beyond feminine influence until seduced by the fictitious and literary, rather than traditional or legendary, sorceress Nimuë or Vivien.

The most potent feminine image in the Merlin tradition is that of Morgen, who is never found as a human being. She is the goddess or priestess of the Otherworld, mistress of shape changing, therapy, and magical flight. It is interesting to note that while Geoffrey embodies certain feminine divine images from tradition into the wife and sister of Merlin, he has no direct contact between Morgen and Merlin. Perhaps the two characters were not directly related in tradition, for Morgen seems to play a major role in the mythical cycle of King Arthur, and is only attached to Merlin in later literary developments. We might simplify this matter by saying that the wounded king is delivered to the goddess or priestess of the Other-world for healing ... but the adventures of Merlin are carried out in the human world in which goddesses are generally found within or through human women.

To state grandly that all feminine characters, personae and archetypes merge in the Goddess is undoubtedly true, but in practical terms we need to be able to distinguish between them. Failure to do so leads to imbalance and confusion, just as in early legends, the converse failure to recognise the Goddess leads to madness.

The true nature of Merlin is mysteriously woven into this matter of recognition of the Goddess or ultimate feminine principle and power. The mystery is not one of faith, dogma or spurious 'occultism' but of perception, poetry and the cycles of myth and legend. Thus there is no rational or complete answer to the question of who Merlin might be ... but one of the ways of seeking such answers is to examine his relationship to Woman.

Merlin and Woman does this in a number of differing ways, some direct, others oblique. While the overall theme of Merlin and Woman is the foundation of this book, there is no predefined rule or method that limits individual contributions. Each writer has devoted time to an aspect of Merlin that he or she presented at the Conference. These range from detailed examinations of Celtic myth and legend to stories created and improvised in performance ... and such stories do not necessarily include the character of Merlin.

One of the curious results of the theme of Merlin and Woman is a repeated emphasis upon seership or prophecy that runs through each contribution to the book. While no specific decision was made to examine the nature of seership or individual seers and prophets in Western literature art or esoteric tradition, the subject is unavoidable in the context of Merlin and Woman.

The remarkable *Prophecies of Merlin* (twelfth century) contain key images of goddesses, both of the land and of the stellar realms; it seems likely that these verses are derived from an early source in which a goddess inspires the bard or seer, just as the historical thirteenth-century seer Thomas Rhymer was inspired by the mysterious Fairy Queen. Thus we have three strands woven together in this book: Merlin and Woman, Story Telling, and Prophecy. The three may not be fully separated, for each partakes of the other. In the context of prophecy, it must be stressed that mere prediction is not of any great value; trivial nonsense regarding mundane prediction is published daily, and forms no part of the deeper traditions associated with Merlin. The importance of prophecy lies in changes of awareness, in inspiration, in alternative visions of potential reality;

prophecy is closely woven with poetry while prediction is usually the poorest level of prose.

Contributions are not limited to specific references to Merlin; indeed, two chapters, by Gareth Knight and Kathleen Raine respectively, deal with major figures in Western tradition and history: Dr John Dee and William Blake. While Dee was a mathematician and scientist, and Blake was a poet and visionary artist, both were deeply involved in the arts of prophecy or seership allied to spiritual or higher consciousness. Achieving this higher consciousness is one of the clearly defined aims of the Merlin tradition ... in which humans seek awareness that flies beyond time, space and events in pursuit of truth.

Neither the Conference nor the book has lost sight, however, of the value of Merlin as an exemplar or entertaining character within a cycle of tales. When Geoffrey of Monmouth wrote his famous Merlin texts, he was not concerned with preserving ancient traditions but with generating a good entertaining set of verses and tales, improving, as he saw it, upon the bardic entertainments with which he was familiar from Breton and Welsh culture. If we limit Merlin and related traditions to arid studies of comparative literature, we lose sight entirely of the great mystery, charm and imaginative transformation contained in the tales themselves. This magical quality overflows into historical persons also; the life of John Dee, for example, is one of the most fascinating adventure stories ever told, while that of William Blake is one of the classic examples of a human being upholding spiritual truth in defiance of material values.

If we are to make any judgement upon what Merlin has to offer the twentieth and twenty-first centuries, the answer may be a recovery of the art of story telling, of the imagination as a shared power of transformation, rather than a pallid replay of media stimuli. The prophecies, cosmology and strong emphasis upon feminine qualities or energies that are all inseparable from the figure of Merlin act as corrective and revivifying influences upon our imagination. Before proceeding to our chapters containing the various contributions to the 1987 Conference, we should first examine the concept of 'Merlin and Story Telling' in greater detail.

1 For English texts, detailed commentary, and discussions of personae and symbols see: *Mystic Life of Merlin* and *Prophetic Vision of Merlin*, R. J. Stewart: Arkana, 1986, London and Boston, Mass.

PART 1
MERLIN AND STORY TELLING

Merlin and Story Telling
by R. J. Stewart

Story telling was a feature of the Second Merlin Conference. Contributors read stories from their books or unpublished material and also improvised tales (often with suprising results) before an attentive audience. Stories were told by a wide range of tellers and methods, beginning with improvisations by film director John Boorman, followed by John Matthews, myself, and an unnamed person who stepped out of the audience and told a vivid tale of prehistory and ritual sacrifice. One of the improvised tales was taken up by Rachel Pollack, who added to it and expanded upon it, whereupon a number of connectives were made by other tale tellers with hilarious results. Much of this was a matter of the moment, of performance, and would not necessarily work in written form.

At the opposite extreme, masterly contributions were made by Peter Vansittart and Peter Dickinson, each reading from his published or soon to be published works to an attentive theatre audience; and between improvisation and formal inspired writing came one of the more curious story-telling arts which is now reappearing in the twentieth century. Rachel Pollack created a story (see Part 4) by drawing a pattern of tarot cards. This method of using tarot is perhaps the true essence of such images, and the relatively modern methods of 'fortune telling' are really derivatives of the primal image-generating and story-telling function of the cards.

At the 1987 Conference I described the creation of the Merlin Tarot, a modern set of images drawing upon the Merlin texts in general, and the *Vita* and *Prophecies* (twelfth century) in particular. The main conclusion from such research is that tarot is derived from a broad tradition of poetic images, used in recreating legends and heroic sagas such as were known in early cultures.

The adventures of Merlin form such a cycle of legends and are clearly defined through tarot images. Thus there is a relationship between the character of Merlin and the art of story telling which is far deeper and more potent than the repeated use of Merlin or similar 'magician' characters in modern fiction.

Merlin was, of course, a story teller. In the *Prophecies* we find him relating the story of the future history of Britain, and finally describing the apocalyptic (but not orthodox Christian) end of the universe. No greater story exists, and as Merlin foresaw all things, he therefore knows all stories. We find this aspect of Merlin portrayed strongly in John Boorman's film *Excalibur*, where the prophet is almost bored by human endeavour, but deeply shocked when the bright spirit of young Arthur steps beyond the frame of the original story and so creates a new branch of reality or a new world.

On a more historical level, we know that Merlin, as a title, person or legend, is somehow involved in bardic arts. It seems very likely that Geoffrey of Monmouth, almost the first writer to set out the Merlin legends and prophecies from oral tradition, drew much of his material from Welsh or Breton bards. Thus Merlin was originally found within an oral organic tradition of tale telling, and this is where the images now known as 'tarot' come into the picture.[1] Such images, deriving from myth, legend and the Elemental world-view of ancient cultures, were the basic substance of the Merlin tales.

There is evidence for the use of images ... creation of pictures in connection with story telling, from twentieth-century sources. A Scottish story teller described to researcher D. A. Macdonald how he remembered the long Gaelic tales and sagas not through detailed application of word learning, but through a sequence of images which he projected 'upon the wall'.[2] This is the true origin of tarot in essence, though without the metaphysical sophistication of the Four Elements, Three Worlds, and other attributes which are so clearly found in the twelfth-century Merlin texts.

Such proven texts predate the first formal tarot packs by three hundred years, and similarly predate the *Triumphs* of Petrarch which are frequently assumed to be the main source of 'trumps' or 'triomphi'.[3]

We have, therefore, a series of connectives. Merlin saw the entire story of the future, yet certain acts may change the flow of this prevision and surprise the seer. Likewise *images* play an important part in oral tale telling and preservation; by the Renaissance period formal sets of images were preserved as picture cards, inspired in Italy by the works of a master poet, but not by any means exclusively derived from these works, as we find the same images and systems in proven earlier texts relating to Merlin. Finally, the formal sets of images, tarot, were used traditionally in Europe by story tellers to generate the basis of tales from patterns of key pictures and meanings; likewise the tarot were used to tell the story of any person's life ... hence the predictive value.

Prediction is not predestination, however, and just as a crude card 'reading' cannot define an individual future rigidly, so do the *Prophecies of Merlin* contain many regenerative themes and images which can alter the future through magical or spirtual means.

The two extremes, personal and universal, are to a certain extent fused together in the *Vita Merlini*, in which a complex cycle of tales, incorporating metaphysics, cosmology and cosmography focuses upon the travels of Merlin around the Wheel of Life. Eventually, aided by his sister Ganieda, he transcends interaction or fate and becomes spiritually mature.

Little wonder that story telling should be associated with Merlin, not merely through the roots of tarot found in the medieval Merlin texts, but in his role as primal prophet of the land, teller of the great story of all life.

The Merlin Conference began as an event in which a small number of specialist authors read and published papers on aspects of Merlin in literature and tradition which were not generally known. Within a year this expanded into a combination of talks, drama, film and story telling. The expansion was not one of ambition, but of inevitable growth from the primal roots of the Merlin tradition.

If we are to restore Merlin to a proper place in the imagination, rather than relegate him to the dreary stereotype of the pseudo-wise elder (so beloved of both academics and spiritualists), we need to allow him space to tell his own tale.

No social gathering, of course, can possibly contain that tale, for it runs from the Creation of the Land to the End of the Solar System, as described in the *Prophecies*. Between these extremes there is a vast cycle of adventures found in the *Vita* and later Arthurian texts, with many modern restatements still appearing. Similarly no single book or series of books can represent Merlin's tale, for much of it has not yet happened as far as we are concerned; but we can gather together various stories, researches, and insights, all of which help us to attune to the greater mystery or the Great Story. The secret is in the blending of research, evidence, and imagination; and this is a type of alchemy which has been sought out by the various contributors to this second 'Book of Merlin'.

NOTES TO MERLIN AND STORY TELLING

1 See R. J. Stewart *The Merlin Tarot* (book and full-colour set of cards), illustrated by Miranda Gray, Aquarian Press, 1988.
2 D. A. Macdonald and Alan Bruford, *Memory in Gaelic Story-telling,* in *Offprints from Scottish Studies,* Vol. 22, University of Edinburgh, 1978.
3 G. Moakley *The Tarot Trumps and Petrarch's Trionfi* in *Bulletin of New York Public Library,* Vol. 60, No. 2, February 1956. For a clear summary of Renaissance tarot see *The Tarot Trumps,* John Shepherd, Aquarian Press, 1985.

The 'Merlin Tarot'

by R. J. Stewart
Cosmology and psychology in the Vita Merlini and Merlin legends

More nonsense has been written, published, taught and practised in connection with tarot than with any other traditional symbolic subject. Indeed much of the recent material offered on tarot seems to bear only the most superficial connection to any tradition whatsoever, and serves to trivialise a subject already maligned and confused in the general imagination. Tarot books and tarot packs are dashed off on the weakest (yet commercialised) pretexts; rampant gushing enthusiasm over tarot clashes with evangelistic condemnation ... neither extreme seems to have any clear idea of what tarot really represents.

In the light of this situation, which perhaps reflects some insight upon our culture in general, Miranda Gray and I have had the daunting task of presenting and justifying the 'Merlin Tarot'. The twenty-two trumps were shown on a large screen at the 1987 Merlin Conference, and the following summary is based upon my own talk supporting the images.

The physical creation of the Merlin Tarot consisted of several years of research on my part, preparation of crude sketches and detailed written descriptions for each card, and the gradual assembly of a cosmology and psychology drawn from early tradition, mainly represented by the *Vita Merlini* written around 1150 by Geoffrey of Monmouth, who drew from existing traditions and texts for much of his material. My source material and imagery was then translated into pencil sketches by Miranda Gray, and after some discussion and correction (surprisingly little, as it happened) she proceeded with colour painting.

My reasons for generating the Merlin Tarot were complex, but rested primarily upon the simple fact that a coherent tradition of images exists in the Merlin texts: this tradition predates the earliest known tarot cards by at least three centuries, and yet many tarot trumps and tarot patterns based upon an Elemental world-view are found therein.

The most sound theory, to date, for tarot origins has perhaps been that ascribing them to the *Triumphs* of Petrarch, but in the *Vita* and *Prophecies* we have earlier proven dated texts employing tarot trump imagery. We also have a mystical philosophy similar to that which flourished during the Renaissance in connection with tarot, alchemy, and other magical or Hermetic arts and sciences. In other words, Geoffrey of Monmouth, Petrarch and many other poets over a period of three centuries or more, adapted a flourishing set of traditions to their own individual creative ends. It should not surprise us in any way that tarot imagery is found within such adaptations, for tarot is merely a formalised symbolic tradition ... a collection of images and patterns.

Tarot is not, and never has been, defined by the history of painted or printed cards: this aspect is merely that of factual dating of *objects*. Such dating is essential and valuable, particularly when it comes to deflating the nonsense written about tarot in connection with popular nineteenth- and twentieth-century occultism; but it does not help us in any way towards an understanding of tarot and its origins. To this end, texts such as the poems of Petrarch (his series of *Triumphs*) and the much earlier Merlin material formalised by Geoffrey of Monmouth are of far greater value than any arguments over the dating or ordering of tarot as cards.

If we are to understand tarot, we must approach it as an organic tradition, something which has an imaginative life, and which appears and reappears in the collective imagination, becoming formalised only by specific writers, story tellers, poets or artists.

Many tarot books and packs fall short simply because they do not come from this organic imaginal tradition: they are instead based upon notions or superficially attractive concepts, rather like any party game or temporary fashion. Conversely we have several highly intellectual, pan-philosophical and multi-cultural religious tarot books and decks; these are at first more satisfying to the mind, as they demonstrate real thought and effort on the part of their creators

... but traditions cannot be fused and transcended upon paper, they must be experienced directly and absorbed into consciousness.

WHAT IS THE MERLIN TAROT?

The Merlin Tarot is a modern attempt to represent primal images found in the Merlin texts; by the simple act of assembling them and redefining them for visual imaginative use, such images become a 'tarot'. But there is more to the Merlin Tarot than this initial formalising of images, for many of the specific images now known to us through tarot cards dating from the Renaissance period are clearly described in the much earlier Merlin texts. Such description falls into three interpenetrating categories:

1) Individual images which correspond directly to standard tarot trumps or other tarot cards
2) Elemental Systems shared by many world views prior to the rise of materialist science
3) Mystical vision of Three Worlds based upon metaphysical states represented by the Moon, Sun and Stars.

Each of these three categories is shared by the *Vita Merlini*, related Merlin texts and traditions, and by basic tarot as defined by the appearance of formal painted or printed cards. Yet, as stated above, a period of three centuries divides the Merlin texts and the Renaissance cards, with a number of poetical and literary sources in between which might reasonably be said to represent tarot-like traditions.

It has frequently been noted that prior to Geoffrey of Monmouth there was very little written concerning King Arthur, but that once his *History of the British Kings* appeared in the middle of the twelfth century, a veritable flood of Arthurian material followed. Geoffrey's *History*, however, like his Merlin texts, was drawn from a collective oral and partly literary tradition ... he did not simply sit down and make it all up. When later writers developed from Geoffrey's texts, they too drew from various traditions and sources known to them. Thus we could take any coherent branch of these poetical-historical traditions and find, quite legitimately and without recourse to coy occult speculation, remnants of ancient mystical and magical world views.

In defining the Merlin Tarot, however, I resisted the temptation to be inclusive: there are no intellectual attempts to incorporate Arthurian legend into the images and their system, and no vaguely nationalistic or revival-pagan attempts to include Celtic deities. That the Celtic deities are present in the Merlin Tarot is undeniable ... but this is due to their fundamental presence within the Merlin tradition, rather than any formal juggling of correspondences on my part or by Miranda Gray during her painting.

As far as Arthurian legends are concerned, the primal Merlin tales predate the Arthurian corpus, as does the mystical world view that lives deep at the very roots of symbolic texts such as the *Prophecies* and *Vita*. No matter how much we assume from modern fiction, a simple examination of the Merlin texts and early legends will show, perhaps surprisingly to many readers, that there was little or no connection between Merlin and Arthur before or even in the works of Geoffrey of Monmouth. All that came later in literary ramifications; one of the most interesting aspects of the Merlin Conferences has been to clarify publicly this entire matter from both an academic and poetic or symbolic viewpoint.

Merlin is associated with Arthur through the ancient traditions of Celtic druidism, bardism, and the role of kingship advised by magical wisdom; but Merlin also has a full and powerful set of traditions entirely his own; those of his personal life, development, insights, prophetic visions, and transformative experiences. These are nothing to do with Arthur, and most of them occur before Arthur is born or before he comes to the throne.

While Arthur represents the once and future king (or all true kings) Merlin represents the enduring traditions of magical transformation and esoteric wisdom. I might add that we do not necessarily have to 'believe' in such traditions as being totally true and effective, but we cannot deny that they span many centuries of cultural experience and that they have validity in many ways ranging from simple belief, educational preservation and dissemination of knowledge, to mystical insight or religious experience.

When assembling and redefining the Merlin Tarot, I relied on clear

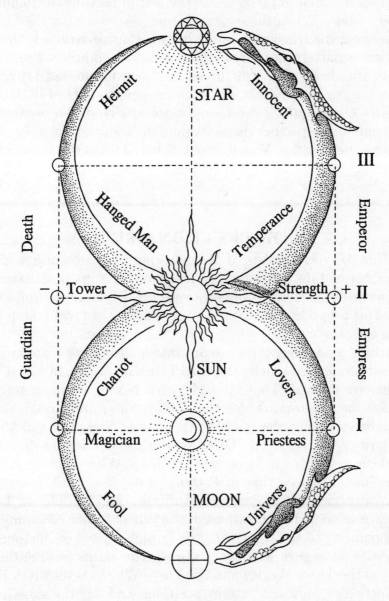

Figure 1   *The Worlds, Dragons and Trumps, from* The Merlin Tarot

I. Lunar World   II. Solar World   III. Stellar World
(First Wheel)   (Second Wheel)   (Third Wheel)

25

and powerful images preserved in the Merlin texts as the foundation of the system. When these images were placed within the Creation Vision described in such detail in the *Vita Merlini* by the bard Taliesin, a pattern appeared which not only completed the Merlin Tarot, but threw new light upon the basic formalised tarot decks which are our first evidence of such imagery as sets of illustrations or cards. Once again, I must emphasise, the tradition predates and underpins any specific visual examples. To grasp this we should examine the Creation Vision, which is based upon the ancient metaphysical concepts of Three Worlds and Four Elements.

THE CREATION VISION

The *Vita Merlini* consists of Merlin's spiralling adventures around the Wheel of Life, encountering the Four Seasons both externally and inwardly as changes of consciousness, personality, and experience. This progress corresponds, of course, to the tarot trump of the *Wheel of Fortune*.

Merlin's mad adventures are put into a cosmic context through a triple vision offered him by the bard Taliesin, a vision in which Three Worlds are defined. These Worlds, each having limits of influence and specific inhabitants, are the Stellar, Solar and Lunar Worlds. They correspond conceptually to the trumps *Star, Sun* and *Moon* in standard tarot decks. The Three Worlds are defined by their limits of influence, which I have termed the Three Wheels.

The lowest Wheel, that of *Fortune*, is the first level, upon which Merlin experiences alternatively suffering and happiness; but he undergoes two further rotations of the Wheel before becoming wise, corresponding to the trumps *Justice* (a higher level of Fortune) and *Judgement* (a higher level of Justice). The harmonic relationship between the Three Worlds and the Three Wheels is shown in Figure 1, which also indicates trump positions and relationships in the overall cosmology and magical psychology of the *Vita*. These relationships can be further equated with the Tree of Life, a metaphysical glyph which appeared in various forms in Europe (from the Middle Ages onwards) through a fusion of native magical tree symbolism with sophisticated mathematical relationships derived from Jewish mysticism and Arabic and Greek philosophical models.

Within this triple cosmology and magical psychology, we find rotations of the Four Elements, and a set of associated archetypes or magical personae which form the familiar trumps of the remainder of the tarot pack. Reference to the *Vita* and to a lesser extent the *Prophecies* and *History* gives us a number of insights into early images from which later tarot developed, and most important of all into the relationships between these images. One of the major problems with any approach to tarot that reaches beyond superficial fortune telling is that of the pattern within which the images (cards) are supposedly assembled.

The Merlin pattern depends upon Three Worlds, Three Wheels and sets of personae within each world that relate harmonically to one another. All of these personae, with the sole exception of the *Hierophant*, are clearly described in the Merlin texts. Thus we have 21 of the 22 trumps, a triple cosmology, and adventures and descriptions that define their roles both individually and with regard to one another. It should be stressed that there is no implication that any pictures were necessarily before Geoffrey of Monmouth as he wrote: the images are embodied within poetry or bardic tradition ... pictures were a later development. Thus we may summarise the personae in each of the Three Worlds without illustrating them individually, and this is found in Table 1. This pattern of relationship may be effectively employed with any tarot pack and gives rise to many concepts in meditation or story telling.

Table 1: Relationships within the Merlin Tarot
Derived from personae and images in the *Vita Merlini, Prophecies of Merlin.*

The Stellar World: The Star, Wheel of Judgement

	Internalising Images	Externalising Images
1	HERMIT (M) ↔	INNOCENT or Hierophant (F)
2	HANGED MAN (M) ↔	TEMPERANCE (F)
3	DEATH (F) ↔	EMPEROR (M)

The Solar World: The Sun, Wheel of Justice

4 BLASTED TOWER (M) ↔ STRENGTH (F)
5 GUARDIAN or DEVIL (M) ↔ EMPRESS (F)
6 CHARIOT (F + M) ↔ LOVERS (M + F)
The Lunar World: The Moon, Wheel of Fortune
7 MAGICIAN (M) ↔ PRIESTESS (F)
8 FOOL (M) ↔ WORLD or UNIVERSE (F)

Short cross-reference to source texts:
Key: *V* = *Vita Merlini*, *P* = *Prophecies of Merlin*, *H* = *History of the Kings of Britain*. (H) only appears in immediate context of (P).
1 = Aged Merlin (*V*) and Divine Child or Maiden (*P*)
2 = Threefold Death (*V*) and Purifier of Land (*P*)
3 = Apple Woman/Morrigan (*V*) and Rhydderch (*V*)
4 = Vortigern's Tower (*H*) and Power of Sovereignty (*P*)
5 = Lord of Animals (*V*) and Lady of Flowers (*V*)
6 = Minerva/Brigidda/'Ganieda' (*V*) and *Lovers* motif (*V*) see 5.
7 = Taliesin/Bladud (*V*/*H*) and Morgen (*V*)
8 = Youth of Three Disguises (*V*) and Universal Creation (*V*) or expressed outer world of Nature (*V*)

STAR SUN MOON/FORTUNE JUSTICE JUDGEMENT are found in the *Creation Vision* (*V*) with JUDGEMENT described in detail in the *Apocalyptic Vision* (*P*)

Further correlations:
1 Archetypes of Wisdom (aged male and divine female)
2 Archetypes of Sacrifice and Grace
3 Archetypes of Taking and Giving or catabolic and anabolic energies. (Correspond in later Arthurian legends to the *Loathly Lady* and *King Arthur*.)
4 Archetypes of destruction and construction of form and environment. (Correspond in later Arthurian legend to the *Wasted Land* and the restorative power of *Sovereignty*.)
5 Archetypes of Hunter and Grower, or male and female keepers and tenders of animals and plants. (Correspond in later Arthurian legend to various *Herdsmen, Giants*, and to *Queen Guenevere*.)
6 Archetypes of culture goddess (intellect) and god of love (emotions): both enable or energise human life patterns. (Correspond in later Arthurian legend to various inspiring or enabling feminine characters who arm or direct knights upon the Quest, and to the motif of Lancelot and Guenevere.

In the *Vita* this motif relates to Merlin and Guendoloena, who are also symbolised individually by the trumps of Guardian and Empress as in 5 above.)

7 Archetypes of magician and priestess in tradition: (corresponds in later Arthurian legend to *Merlin* and to *Morgan le Fey*.) Represent two paths (Hermetic and Orphic) or transforming consciousness within magical or spiritual traditions.

8 Archetypes of essential spirit or human soul, and the Elemental World or Macrocosm and Microcosm of metaphysical teachings. These images are preserved in various Celtic legends and in European ritual folk drama involving death and resurrection ceremonies, a man-woman, and a fool. (Corresponds in later Arthurian legend to *Perceval/Peredur or Galahad* as the Fool, with the World or Universe as the restored *Land* which results from a successful Quest for the Holy Grail.)

TOTEM CREATURES

When the Merlin Tarot trumps were designed, it seemed important to keep some of the unique elements of the Merlin legends in the picture images, elements which are not present in standard tarot. Much of Merlin's cycle of adventures is concerned with totem animals and birds, due to its relationship to the lost *Mabon* cycle in which all orders of creation play a part in the adventures of the Child of Light. Thus most of the trumps in the Merlin Tarot contain totem creatures, each creature having a symbolic traditional relationship to the trump in which it is found. The Two Dragons, featured in our Figure 1, appear in several roles, in addition to acting as a master symbol for the cosmic pattern defined by the Creation Vision itself.

Merlin is often associated with the Wolf, the Hound (or Black Dog), the Stag and the Pig. A sequence of totem animals and birds ranging from the Wren to the Lion appears in the Merlin Tarot trumps. Some of these creatures, such as Dog, Wolf and Lion are important in standard tarot; others derive from the rich stratum of creatures in tradition that leads to an expanded story cycle of the Divine Child and his or her relationship with all created beings.

Frequently the totem creatures in any symbolic picture support the main character or persona, and tell of important sub-traditions or primal themes and beliefs which remain attached to the more sophisticated aspects of the image.

THE NUMBER CARDS

Having progressed thus far, it seemed right to extend the totem creature concept into the Elemental or Number Cards. The Elements of Air, Fire, Water and Earth are represented by Birds, Serpents (or Dragons), Fishes, and Beasts. These are drawn in interlacing patterns, just as the customary Swords, Wands, Cups and Coins are interlaced or balanced in standard tarot. As might be expected, Miranda Gray has drawn the Number Cards in the style of the old Celtic knotwork or interweaving patterns found in early gospels or upon ancient inscribed stones. This is not a mere artifice, for such patterns were of major importance to the Celts, paralleled in the complex digressions, interrelationships and imagery of the Merlin texts themselves.

THE COURT CARDS

The Court Cards become the courts of Birds, Serpents, Fishes and Beasts: the personae are defines as Pages, Warriors, Queens and Kings. Once again the emphasis is upon the Seasons, upon animals and birds, and upon human qualities (Elemental psychology) in association with the powers of nature. This means that the Court Cards are of greater importance in the Merlin Tarot than in many other decks, and act as powerful archetypical images in their own right. Pages are always on foot, and may be male or female; Warriors are on horseback and are female (though they may also be seen as male), while Kings and Queens are clearly defined sexually and sit upon thrones symbolic of the Element to which they attune. The Court Cards are also vital in the *story-telling* role attached to the Merlin Tarot, and are specifically intended to be used for generation

Figure 2   The Guardian from, The Merlin Tarot

of stories in addition to meditation, visualisation and the incidental function of fortune telling.

THE TRUMPS

The entire pack cannot be summarised in a short chapter, but there are several important trumps that are worth describing briefly in the context of restoring tarot in general as a balanced set of symbols. The first three requiring specific discussion are:

1) The Devil
2) Death
3) Judgement

1) *The Devil* becomes the *Guardian* or Lord of the Animals, a role undertaken by Merlin when he reverts to primal nature in his fits of madness. The trump shows a fierce, wild-looking man, naked but for a cloak of green leaves lined with red flames. He wears, or has growing from his head, a set of deer's antlers, and is accompanied by various totem birds and beasts. The Guardian is clearly defined in Celtic tradition, but eventually becomes amalgamated with the Judeo-Christian *shaitan* or adversary and the parallel Greek figure of the great god Pan. This unfortunate fusion of two beneficial temperate-clime pagan deities, Cernunnos and Pan, with a malefic or testing entity from a desert culture resulted in the suppressive image of the Devil or 'false god' still found in tarot cards today.

The original role of Guardian is as a protector of the weak, revealer of the secrets of both inner and outer nature, and as the great initiator or stern psychopomp of the Mysteries. This role is emphasised in the Merlin Tarot, and concepts of suppression, temptation, lust and other negative qualities are absent. In fact the Guardian challenges us to rebalance such weaknesses within ourselves, just as the Celtic Lord of the Animals protects all creatures, sacred wells or sources of power in the land. His image and legend is widespread in folklore, literature and early images from Romano-Celtic culture. (See Figure 2.)

2) *Death* becomes a female figure, standing before an Apple Tree.

Figure 3 Judgement, from The Merlin Tarot

She is the mysterious woman-of-apples who tries to kill Merlin (in the *Vita*) and the Fairy Queen of folklore. In Gaelic tradition she is often known as the *Washer at the Ford*, an entity deriving from the Irish goddess or goddess group known as the *Morrigan*. She is the ancient goddess of death-in-life, one of the major deities of the Celts, and certainly represented in various forms in early texts including the *Prophecies* and the *Vita*. (See Figure 5.) The familiar and nowadays ludicrous dancing skeleton with scythe of standard tarot is derived from this primal European image of a death goddess and her reaping hook ... but with additional propaganda elements related to our next trump, *Judgement*.

3) *Judgement* is drawn from the remarkable apocalypse described in the *Prophecies of Merlin*. A mysterious goddess, called Ariadne, unweaves the Solar System, planet by planet and sign by sign, until only the Four Elements or Winds remain. While doing so she summons the Ancestors from the primal ocean, and is attended by a two-headed or 'Janus' figure, acting as her door keeper. This symbolism is employed in the *Judgement* trump of the Merlin Tarot, replacing the orthodox concept of an angel summoning the elect to resurrection.

Yet the symbolism of both visions is very similar: a summoning figure, the ancestors, the sea, and potential resurrection out of dissolution. Once again, the propaganda element of a state political religion, now alien to the modern consciousness, may be effectively replaced by an early form of a related image. The inner meaning or spirit of the image remains constant, even though the outer form changes in various tarot designs due to pressures from orthodox religion and suppressive dogma. (See Figure 3).

Three further trumps demand special attention in the context of the Merlin Tarot, for they are major characters in both the Merlin legends and the later Arthurian and Grail cycles. Once again it must be stressed that these trumps or archetypical personae, closely related to early pagan god forms and easily identifiable with various characters in both medieval literature and oral tradition, are found *entire* in the *Vita Merlini*, written around 1150. They are not fabrications or exercises in intellectual skill by myself as designer and author or Miranda Gray as artist.

34

Figure 4   The Priestess, from The Merlin Tarot

The second list consists of:

1) The Fool/Hanged Man
2) The Hermit
3) The Priestess

1) *The Fool/Hanged Man*. Although two separate trumps are employed, the *Vita* makes it clear that the Fool and the Hanged Man are the same person at different stages of his life. As the *Fool* he appears in three disguises, an innocent youth who is to become a curious victim of the ritualised Threefold Death. When he falls, hangs and drowns simultaneously as an adult, he becomes the Hanged Man. The entire theme is connected to an ancient ritual religious subject, in which the relationship between humanity and the land is dependent upon the qualities of sacrificial kingship.

In a religious context, the Fool developing into the Hanged Man may be interpreted on both pagan and Christian levels as an ancient sacred king, or as Christ. In a magical or psychological context, the Fool stands for every man and woman setting out upon the quest for truth; the Hanged Man represents that inversion of consciousness or sacrifice of false values necessary to attain enlightenment.

This progression is defined in the *Vita* as a parallel legend linked to the increasing maturity and insight of Merlin himself. We might presume that originally the theme was attached to Merlin or Mabon, who, like the Christian Saviour, transcended mere physical death through spiritual grace. Such a sensitive subject was probably confused or suppressed by the time Geoffrey of Monmouth was writing, however, so the tale parallels that of Merlin without ever stating who the anonymous Youth may be. Only in the Scottish legends of *Lailoken*, also called Merlin, do we find the Threefold Death directly attached to the prophet himself.

As shown in Table 1 (p. 27), the Fool progresses through various stages of enlightenment: Fool/Magician/Guardian/Hanged Man/ Hermit. *En route* he encounters the influences or personae of the Chariot/Blasted Tower and, of course, Death. This is the inward-seeking Path of mystical enlightenment, through progressive stages of dis-enchantment, purgation or catabolic transformation, and sub-

Figure 5   Death, from The Merlin Tarot

sequent regeneration. Significantly, Merlin himself undergoes such painful transformations in the *Vita* (see *Merlin, King Bladud, and the Wheel of Life* in the first *Book of Merlin*).

2) *The Hermit.* This image is clearly described at the close of the *Vita* when the aged Merlin refuses to act as Judge or Druid to the assembled chieftains, but decides to retire to a stellar observatory to contemplate Divinity. Here Merlin is the most aged of aged men, having experienced all things, older than the oldest tree or oldest creature. Once again we find echoes of the Mabon legend in which aged primal beasts lead heroes to their hunt for the sacred Child. It may be significant that this third turning of the Wheel, equating to the trump *Judgement* with qualities of timelessness, understanding, wisdom and final spiritual values, is linked to Merlin's refusal to *judge* the assembled princes or chieftains. The three orders of druids, known as bards, seers or vates, and druids, may equate to the three Wheels and Three Worlds.

3) *The Priestess.* This trump corresponds to the major personae of *Morgen* in the *Vita*, who is mistress of magical flight, shape changing and therapy. She rules the Fortunate Isle, or Avalon, and takes the wounded Arthur under her care. A vast stream of Arthurian litera-ture grew from this single and basic simple Celtic archetype of a primal goddess; many of the curious twists in her career are discussed in other chapters in this book, particularly the erroneous concept that she was an evil or corrupting influence. The original Morgen is a being representing the best qualities of the druidic or primal Celtic goddesses of transformation: she rules the arts with her eight sisters, and her other abilities, such as flight and therapy, are all expressions of transformative, positive beneficial energies (see Figure 4).

To conclude this short exploration of symbolism in the Merlin texts, and the recreation of the Merlin Tarot, we need to consider one further trump: the *Hierophant.* As stated above, this is the only trump that does not have a reasonable archetype or correspondence within the Geoffrey of Monmouth Merlin texts and related Merlin sources.

Initially, I considered that *Taliesin* in his role as preserver and disseminator of cosmology, metaphysics and natural history, was comparable to the role of Hierophant in Renaissance tarot. After all, was he not a wise man who expounded the Mysteries to the mad Merlin? The true nature of the Hierophant or Pope is not an educational one, however: it is to act as the direct mediator of spiritual power. In this sense we find that Taliesin is actually fulfilling the role of *bard* in the strict sense of a preserver and reciter of vast bodies of traditional lore or assembled knowledge.

The Pope or Hierophant trump represents the most senior role in Renaissance tarot: he is the head of the Church, ruling over the Emperor who in turn rules over all lesser kings. Much blood was shed over this hierarchical system, and in standard tarot it represents *order and authority*. Although the origin of papal power is through Apostolic (spiritual) succession, this plays little or no part in the political hierarchy of Church and State which was well established before tarot cards appeared.

The standard concept of Pope or Hierophant, therefore, was a political statement replacing a spiritual or poetical truth; it could not be applied to the bard Taliesin, for he was a preserver of knowledge in poetic form, and neither a direct temporal leader of any organisation nor a perfect spiritual mediator. He relays knowledge that he has learned as a bard, under the tutelage of Minerva, patroness of the arts and sciences.

As is suggested by Figure 1 and Table 1, there is a polarity pattern inherent in the archetypes within tarot, and this pattern of relationships is clearly established through the various stories within the *Vita*. The end of our great tale finds the ancient Merlin, oldest of old and wisest of wise, withdrawing into spiritual contemplation: this is the Hermit, or internalising consciousness at the end of a cycle of time, be it a human life or the life of a star.

To conclude the cycle of the Merlin Tarot, therefore, I chose to replace the orthodox patriarchal political *Hierophant* with a primal image of *Innocence*; but even this change is not a matter of contrivance, for it derives from major cultural and mystical sources.

Popes occasionally take the name 'Innocent' to declare their spiritual grace ... but a primal image of Wisdom has always been feminine. The goddess Sophia takes this role in Gnostic and Greek Christianity, and the *Innocent* of the Merlin Tarot is that originative feminine wisdom which precedes the creation of the worlds. She is, we might say, the spirit that speaks through a true hierophant of the highest Mysteries.

While there is no individual image in the Merlin texts that relates to this ancient and enduring concept, there is a clearly stated set of goddess images as follows:

1) A Maiden appears from an ancient forest
2) She purifies two streams or springs
3) By doing so she becomes mature and immensely powerful holding the forests of Scotland and the towers of London in either hand.

This threefold transformation, from the *Prophecies*, clearly refers to the important concept of the sacred Land and the goddess of Sovereignty found in European tradition and discussed by various authors, particularly in a Celtic and Irish context. It further relates to tarot trumps as follows, in reverse order from manifestation towards inner or spiritual levels, 3) *Strength* 2) *Temperance* 1) (in the Merlin Tarot) the *Maiden or Innocent*.

So this seeming departure from tarot symbolism is not such a departure after all, for it reinstates a feminine aspect and identity to the highest card in the deck. Furthermore this feminine archetype is found clearly described in the *Prophecies* undergoing a triple transformation; in the context of Sovereignty we see it as related to the sanctity of the Land, a subject central to both the *Prophecies* and the *Vita*; but on a higher level or spiral, in the Stellar World, the same triple transformation is an allegory of the creation process of the universe. This triple process, from Stellar to Solar and Lunar Worlds, is exactly the system described in the *Vita*, and counterpointed by the apocalypse of the *Prophecies*.

With this final trump, therefore, which is central to the theme of Merlin and the Goddess, or Merlin and Woman, that runs through the remainder of this book, we can conclude our exploration of some aspects of the Merlin Tarot.

THE CHOICE

by R. J. Stewart
(A story first told at the
1987 Merlin Conference)

Listen, and I will tell of the most frightening monster in the world. It has a power so vast and terrifying that all men and women dread it, avoid it, flee from it. This awful force takes many forms, it pushes us into situations we immediately loathe and regret. It has a strange quality, for we see it clearly while looking backwards over our shoulders, yet it is hardly visible to us when we gaze straight ahead. Heroes, fools, bards and lovers have all wrestled with this giant, to no avail; no mortal man or woman has yet conquered or tamed its harrowing powers.

Even the immortal semi-daemon Merlin fell prey to it in the end, despite a long life leaping far ahead of its pursuing reach, plunging into the tide of inner wisdom to wash his perceptions clean of its confusing influence.

What is this monster? The answer is not hard, and though you might have thought it so, the answer is not death. Seers and mages laugh with death, she is their friend. But even those who have seen the sun at midnight and eaten the sacred apple may cower before the mystery of which I speak. Merlin penetrated far into its depths during his final vision; the Blessed Youth, who has many names and roles, endured certain revelations connected to its terrible inevitable power.

In its greater aspect the mystery appears as a man with two heads, or perhaps a dark man with four heads, whom none may pass unprepared. He is also known as the horned Guardian of thresholds, about whom many strange tales are told. But in its lesser aspect, the power that confronts us from behind has one name only, which we all know well. That name is CHOICE.

Only the fool denies the power of choice over the human spirit, only the fool claims to choose instantly and without regrets. The wise have always chosen badly, regretted deeply ... thus have they found wisdom through outgrowing their regrets. At the beginning of a life there seem to be so many choices, while at the end there were always far too few and those choices recognised were made badly. Yet there is, in truth, only one choice in each lifetime. It manifests in many different ways until the wise man or woman realises the unity of its various identities. The buffoon, wilfully ignorant, of course, persists in false diversity.

It is frequently said that ignorance is a blessing while knowledge is a curse. Far from being trite or trivial this old saw is demonstrated in the story which I am going to tell you. It is the story of someone who had his choice, or rather his Choice, revealed to him in one instant. I leave it to you to judge whether he was blessed or cursed by this gift.

Certain places, especially the ancient centres and homes of human-kind, are not restricted to their outer pattern. In addition to their appearance, such places have an inner topography compounded and vitalised by centuries of endeavour, imagination, and the natural forces of the land itself. Such sites were often chosen for features such as springs, wells, confluence of rivers, all of which carry their reality through time. The successive ages of culture and development interpenetrate one another; we might be walking down a city street but also stepping through an ancient gateway, coexisting (in some superficially earlier century) with our present location. Or by turning the corner of some dull suburb we are also turning within an ancient tale or myth of a local goddess attuned to that very area of land forever.

In some places such myths and histories are well studied, while in others they are mere hints, rumours, and obscure forgotten references. No place reflects this truth more clearly than the ancient city of ... in which the hero, if that is an adequate term to describe him, of our tale once lived. We need only hear of one dream that he had in this city of dreams and chains; when he and he alone out of countless thousands who had dwelt there through the centuries was clearly shown his Choice.

At the time of which I tell, he spent his time in the city, by nature of bonds foolishly accepted. They may have been the simple but potent ties of employment, debt, fidelity and family. Perhaps they were the intangible but corrosive bonds of desire, dream and myth-pollution. Whatever the bonds, they seemed, to our man, to be laid out upon the map of the city itself, reaching into the surrounding lands. As he walked to and fro he seemed to be pacing out the limits of his inner bondage, through a strange landscape that mirrored, yet also defined, whatever was shown upon the mundane street map.

If this still seems unclear, we may consider it in terms of his dreams. In dreams he walked through a landscape and met curious beings; he followed the hidden ways of underground streams; he found the secrets of ancient stones that were openly visible in the outer waking city. He learned about the interaction of space and time with human history, and how each age nourished its own slavery, delusion, imprisonment. Nor was he exempt.

For some years our man had been trying unsuccessfully to reach beyond the city boundaries in his dreams. He had a regular beat, so to speak, in which he knew that a certain type of sleep would carry him so far and no further. A light nap, for example, might take him no more than a few streets from where he slept. He might encounter the phantom of an early Christian church commingling with the ugliness of a large modern store. A long afternoon sleep would carry him spiralling to an ancient temple boundary, where the charm houses of the Roman period prostitutes were consubstantial with the vast modern block filled with computers. In his dream he might watch the girls painting their palms and soles, or trying new per-fumed oils in their hair; perhaps this sensual energy was the cause of the endless computer errors in his own time. A drunken stupor, however, would plunge him down to where certain curious and over-friendly beings lived, desperate for visitors in the dark.

But try as he might, our prisoner, free to roam through time in the dream world, could not make his way beyond defined boundaries. These were marked by the curve of a river, the shape of the under-ground water table, and the rise of some gently sloping hills. Not a hard bondage, you might say, especially if you cannot recall any such dream travelling yourself. Remember that his dream bondage

43

reflected his real enslavement, which was every bit as bad as your own, and perhaps worse.

It was during one particular dream, arising in the cool lucid hour of the earliest dawn, that he finally made a strenuous effort and broke free. It seemed to him that as he slept, he watched the last stars fading, until for a short time the Sun and Moon stood equal in the sky. The Moon paled as the Sun increased its colour in glory over the tip of the distant hill. The ice blue light of the sky gave our prisoner strength within his maze-bound spirit; pointing his nose at the Sun, he began in his dream, to run.

As he ran it seemed that a woman in a slight, short, silver tunic ran with him. She was effortless and long limbed, while he gasped and laboured and stumbled. As she ran, she paced him, encouraged him, her clean, stern face giving him new strength and confidence in himself; but as the Sun increased, she slowly faded away, leaving him at the very point beyond which he had never been able to cross.

Filling his heaving chest with air, he flung himself onwards in one great desperate effort. Houses, roads, trees, hedges, all flew aside to let him pass. Time compressed, the Sun stood still upon his rising, and our runner emerged through a tunnel of confluence to fall gasping down upon green grass. The coolness and freshness of this grass flowed through the hot palms of his hands and the sweating side of his face. He lay there drawing energy from the smell of it, earthy and green as the world was when it first came to birth. He knew that he had broken free at last.

Yet try as he might he could not at first stand upright. It was as if this vital earth drew him down like a lover, and would not allow him to pull away. He finally forced himself up with his arms, passing from a crouching position to an upright one. His back began to ache.

As is always the case with escaped prisoners, he first looked not around him nor ahead, but over his shoulder. In the distance the smouldering city lay under an orange haze, red glow pulsing in its secret corrupt heart. It nestled at the end of a long tunnel into which many roads wound and merged, yet none led to the place in which he now stood. Perhaps he was safe from pursuit. For a moment after this comforting thought he was puzzled as to how he had arrived in

Figure 6   The Runner

such a green place. Then he remembered his foot race with the silver maiden and his longing to break free.

Now he looked about him. He stood upon a small flat area roughly circular in shape. The grass was thick yet short, almost as level as a well-kept lawn. Here and there it speckled alive with tiny white flowers; in the distance rising hills formed a double curve guarding a winding road. The road emerged from somewhere beyond the little grass plain, but no entrance could be seen from where he stood. Our escapee discovered that he was just on the edge of the grass, towards the city. Between himself and the centre stood large rough standing stones forming a ring about the perimeter. The stones were between him and the intriguing road ahead.

As he pondered over the stones, debating whether they were set up to the shape of the grassy lawn or the lawn moulded to the shape of the stone circle, he realised that he was not alone. Standing to his right, and slightly behind him, was an old man in a simple robe. He looked like a monk or hermit, his robe tied with a heavy black cord, his hair cut into a curious tonsure, shaven at the front and falling long behind.

'So you seem to have arrived...' murmured the elder, and indicated with a wave of his arm the stone circle. Robed figures stepped out silently from behind each stone, their hoods shadowing their faces.

'As you seem to have arrived,' continued the elder with firm authority, 'You may as well know that we can give you your Choice.' As he spoke a few tiny stars urged through the blueness of morning sky, or perhaps the sky darkened a little to reveal stars already present.

At first these seven stars seemed to draw upon our hero, but the subtle change of light had already revealed a figure within the very centre of the grassy stone circle. Her most enthralling feet resting lightly and well shaped upon the green, with hardly a blade bending under her weight or a flower pushed aside by her toes.

She was young, with long, flowing dark hair of a blue-black lustre shining and rippling like the rivers of night in flood. Her face was of an ivory colour tinged with a gentle shade of rose about her cheeks; her mouth was wide with dark blood-flushed lips. Her nose was strong and narrow, balancing her high cheeks. Her eyes were of deep radiant violet colour, and they looked across the short space towards her enthralled and goggling observer. She wore a long gown of dark blue embroidered with a theme of woven green leaves and red fruit; around the hem of this robe hung tiny silver bells alternate with golden balls. She moved not a hairsbreadth, but if she had moved, she would have filled the circle with flashing and ringing. Her hands were at rest, palms open, long elegant fingers poised . . . she wore no rings.

As the dreamer stared at her he felt that the stars, suddenly revealed above, had come so close that he might simply reach out and touch them.

'Well, there it is . . .' said the old man, turning away, already leaving. He walked upright, holding in his left hand a long staff with coiled serpents carved about it.

Brought to his senses momentarily by such an abrupt departure, our athlete called out hoarsely: 'What? What is it? I don't understand . . .'

The old man turned back, frowning slightly, or perhaps he was smiling in a predatory manner. For a moment it seemed that he would not reply, but he suddenly laughed aloud and said: 'We give you this Choice, the only one that you have in this life. You may have the power of the stars or the love of the princess.' And he strode off rapidly around the left-hand side of the stone-circled green.

It need hardly be stated that the runner had fallen instantly deeply in love with the maiden who stood within that circle. Yet he was also drawn by the power that radiated from the constellation revealed above the land. Unable to choose, he felt the star power twitch within his bones where tiny crystals muttered; but the woman-love burned in his blood and made his throat constrict. As he dithered the robed figures began a curious twisting dance around the circle. He knew that the gathering was ended. As he pondered they increased their speed, turning inwards in a leap as each one passed a stone. For a moment he seemed to see salmon leaping out of green water, then his eye was caught by the distant black figure of the old man striding off towards the hills, not looking back.

As the runner procrastinated, the sun rose higher and the grass gave off a dewy mist. The robed figures began to fade and dissolve, and the stones were enshrouded. Then the fierce sun burned his eyes, intent on driving him forth; the circle was empty as the mist evaporated. As our man hesitated, so he became lost. The scene transformed into an ordinary field which he knew, just outside the city boundary.

Still in his dream, he turned around, dejected, and walked back through the dirty suburbs towards the busy streets. Good citizens scurried to work, or sat patiently in their fume-ridden cars waiting for a chance to move. The timescape did not change, but remained locked in the present. He knew that somehow he had plunged himself deeper into prison; a choice failed was an anchor into time and place that would not easily be lifted.

When he awakened, and when he came awake for all the countless days that followed in that place, the city in which he lived was no different from the city of which he dreamed.

PART 2
MABON

MABON

Oh do you know, or have you heard
Of Mabon, Modron's son,
Who from his mother's womb was reeved
When time was first begun?

Song of Mabon: Caitlín Matthews

Have you found, my soul, what you were seeking? You were seeking
God, and you found him to be that which is the highest of all,
than which a better cannot be thought; you found him to be life itself,
light, wisdom, goodness, eternal blessedness and blessed eternity, and
to exist everywhere and always.

Proslogion: St Anselm of Bec

Introduction

by R. J. Stewart

In the following chapter we are fortunate to have advance material from Caitlín Matthews' forthcoming book *Arthur and the Sovereignity of Britain*, which will be published in 1989 by Arkana. This forms the second volume to her two-part study of the *Mabinogion*, those ancient Welsh tales from enduring legendary tradition.

Her first volume, *Mabon and the Mysteries of Britain*, published in 1987, dealt in detail with the theme of the Celtic divine child; in the same year Geoffrey Ashe, writing in the first *Book of Merlin* (Blandford Press) identified Merlin, Mabon and the primal god of Britain with one another. Prior to both of these discussions and explorations, I had published in 1986 a comparison of Merlin and Mabon, particularly in the context of a lost story involving humans and animals, in *The Mystic Life of Merlin* (Arkana, 1986). There seem to be many shared elements in both Geoffrey of Monmouth's *Vita Merlini* and the shamanistic or totem animal themes in Celtic legends that may relate to the divine child Mabon, a type of Celtic Apollo.

With this steady development of interest in, and exposition of, the role and archetype of the elusive Mabon, it seemed that time was ripe for a specific contribution on the subject at the 1987 Merlin Conference. We might add to our list one aspect of the controversial work of Professor Barry Fell, who claims that inscriptions to 'Mabo-Mabon' written in *ogham* script upon stone, have been found in ancient sites on the east coast of America (*America BC*, Barry Fell: Pocket Books, USA).

Is it possible that Mabon was in fact a major pre-Christian deity, the Celtic Child of Light, and that his cult was extensively developed through Europe, and perhaps found even across tne Atlantic, due to the presence of Celtic settlers? It seems unlikely, even if the American evidence is finally accepted, that we shall never know the true status of Mabon, for his legend bears all the negative signs of having been heavily edited or perhaps at one time banned, for religious propagandist reasons.

Yet enough remains, as Caitlín Matthews shows so effectively in the following chapter, to suggest the nature of Mabon and his primal tale. Mabon relates to the youthful Merlin who prophesied before King Vortigern, and in archetypical symbolic terms Mabon, young Merlin, and the child Apollo are virtually identical. Once again, we are dealing with resonances of a primal prophetic and religious tradition, and with various figures representing that tradition within specific cultures or periods of time. We shall find in Part 6 that William Blake took up this prophetic theme, recreating in his own symbolic language the primal imagery of the powers of the land and the transformation of awareness that is possible when humans and land become attuned properly to one another.

MABON, THE CELTIC DIVINE CHILD

by Caitlín Matthews

Of the many archetypes in Celtic mythology, one of the most intriguing and evasive is that of Mabon, the Celtic Divine Child. In *Mabon and the Mysteries of Britain*[1], I have identified many of the characters within the Mabinogion who manifest the Mabon archetype, but here I would like to range more widely and examine the evidence from a broader basis.

The core of Mabon's identity and function is embedded deeply in Celtic and Arthurian tradition and was obviously well known to earlier oral tradition, if the fragmentation of his archetype is anything to go by. Traces of his story appear in folk tradition and medieval romance. In the aptly named Breton text, the *Roman du Silence*[2], there is a reference to two minstrels performing the *lai Mabon*, attesting to an extant medieval story. Unfortunately, the minstrels are not permitted to give us any verses in this text. Similarly a manuscript of the Shrewsbury School[3] speaks of a *lai* entitled *Rey Mabun* but is as taciturn as the *Roman du Silence*. It is almost as though Mabon's story was so well known and ubiquitous that it is tacitly assumed the story bore no further repetition.

How a British Celtic archetype became the subject of a Breton *lai* is perhaps something we will never be able to trace with any exactitude. Where literary tradition takes over from oral tradition, written evidence runs out and we turn to archaeological backup. Mabon is the local name of the Romano-British deity, Maponus, to whom many dedications have been found in Northern Britain, especially along Hadrian's Wall and the area of the Solway Firth.[4] The characteristics of the British deity in the centuries before Rome may only be guessed at, but he certainly equated, in the Roman mind, with aspects of Apollo and Orpheus.[5] It is possible, though there is little evidence for this, that Maponus was the focus of a minor mystery cult among his Romano-British devotees. Closely associated with Maponus was the cult of the Matres, the Triple Mothers: a fact which should not suprise us, since Mabon is universally called Mabon, son of Modron – Son, son of Mother. The twin cults of Modron and Mabon were undoubtedly ancient before their Classical overlay, and it is this primal tradition which we shall attempt to reconstruct.

The names Mabon and Modron are really titles, not personal names. They are remnants of a mystery tradition where these titles were applied to great divine archetypes, in much the same way Demeter and Kore in Greek tradition have no personal appellation but are known as Mother and Maiden. This custom pertained in Celtic countries where heroes and chieftains swore a variation on this carefully phrased oath: 'I swear by the gods which my tribe swears by'. Such a formula obviated the use of a name. This caution sprang from the reverent custom of concealing the deity's name from the irreverent or uninitiated. Even today, the devout speak of 'Our Lord' and 'Our Lady' rather than the more familiar Jesus and Mary. It is possible that in the pre-Roman era one might have wandered the length and breadth of Britain swearing 'by the Son and his Mother' without any loss of understanding, each tribe holding a Mother and Son in reverence. Indeed one might so swear today without any blasphemous intention.

It is this central premise that we must bear in mind that the titles, Mabon and Modron, are applicable to various youths and their mothers, though certainly not arbitrarily and without warrant. This game of substitution can be played only with a select set of mythic pieces which bear traces of the original archetypes.

The earliest textual reference to the myth of Mabon appears in *Culhwch and Olwen*, one of the many stories appearing in a medieval compilation called the *Mabinogion*.[6] In this story, Culhwch falls in love with a giant's daughter, Olwen, but in order to win her he is set 39 impossible tasks by Olwen's father, Yspaddaden. Chief among these tasks is the finding of Mabon. Culhwch is one of the oldest stories of the *Mabinogion*, stemming from an oral tradition which has its roots in the period immediately following that of the Dark-Age Arthur, *c*537 AD. It embodies traces of ancient often lost stories once prominent in proto-Celtic tradition. The story teller gives a

Figure 7   Mabon and the Creatures of the Land

version of Mabon's story which betrays the manner in which a once-potent myth can be smoothed into folk-tale.

When Culhwch asks for information about Mabon he is told that the child was taken from between his mother and the wall when he was three nights old and that no one knows where he is now, nor indeed whether he is alive or dead. Mabon has departed from the memories of mankind, but the memories of animals prove more retentive, and it is to the animal kingdom that Culhwch directs his search. With him on this quest is Gwrhyr, an interpreter of animal's speech. They start with the blackbird.

The blackbird has not heard of Mabon, though she has pecked an iron anvil down to its wooden base, and she passes them on to the stag of the plains. He remembers a single sapling which grew to be a mighty tree, but even that has withered. He sends them on to the owl of the wood who has seen the triple growth and uprooting of the forest, but has never heard of Mabon. She passes them on to the eagle who has pecked the stars from the heights of a mountain until it is only a few feet high. He has never heard of Mabon, but has rumour of something via a salmon with whom he once battled. The salmon has never heard of Mabon but has been troubled by a crying from the walls of Caer Loyw (Gloucester). The heroes mount on the salmon's back and are led to the walls where they ask the mystery question: 'Oh who is it that there laments within a house of stone?'[6]

They receive the answer: 'It is Mabon, born of Modron's womb, within these walls alone.' Mabon is then brought out on Cai's back and liberated to help Culhwch fulfil the rest of his impossible tasks which will qualify him to marry Olwen.

In this story Mabon is very much a subsidiary character: a famous archetype which the story teller has inserted into the narrative in order to give Culhwch his place among the older heroes. Much the same happens in later medieval romance, where Arthur occasionally makes a guest appearance in order to give the story authenticity within the Matter of Britain.

Nevertheless, the story teller has preserved many elements of Celtic belief and practice. The long search through the agency of animals is closely associated with the transformatory sequence which most Celtic poets boast of having undergone. The poets Amergin[7] of

Ireland and Taliesin[8] of Britain both claim to have inhabited various shapes. This must not be taken to mean a literal shape-shifting, any more than it necessarily implies a reincarnational memory.[9] More precisely, these poets speak of an initiatory sequence of realisations which every initiate of the bardic mysteries undergoes. In that moment of revelation, a complex web of imagery is presented in one vision. Like Celtic knotwork, everything in this vision is connected, leading to further interpretation. It may be the work of a lifetime to comprehend this sequence, which is really a visionary glyph of knowledge.

Forming a chain back to the beginning of time, the animals of Mabon's search each represent a species of knowledge and a non-linear age of time. Encoded both within these beasts and in the story of Mabon's finding is an inner history, an encyclopedia of information and a direct experience of the worlds – both human and otherwordly. This chain of information is borne out from an evolutionary point of view, where each species of animals is part of life's history, each bearing some part of the genetic pattern of creation.

This, then, is the major source for Mabon's extant myth. We find other traces in the Welsh *Triads*,[10] the mnemonic verses which encapsulate sets of knowledge. Triad 52 speaks of Mabon as being one of three famous prisoners.[11] Both the *Mabinogion* and the *Triads* preserve the most persistent part of Mabon's mythos – that he is imprisoned and released. Both these texts are the last remaining links with the tradition of Mabon as a native deity rather than the literary character which he later becomes. They retain his numinous power though neither is as informative as we would like them to be. Taking these texts alone, the paucity of evidence does not help us reconstruct, in even partial fashion, the lost myth of Mabon.

We are fortunate that the Mabon archetype found a vehicle of transmission which showed no signs of abating its progress: Arthurian legend. Any character lodged in the tales which comprise the Matter of Britain has been gifted with the kind of immortality associated with the ancient gods and heroes of British tradition. But what of Mabon? Is it possible to reconstruct something of his original mythos with any certainty? It is certain that the full power of Mabon's archetype has been lost to us, but it is likely that a once-potent god-form such as the Wondrous Child might have left notable traces.

As Alwyn and Brinley Rees have stated in *Celtic Heritage*: 'traditional tales used to be transmitted by a priestly order in the Celtic lands, and diverse blessings accrued to those who heard them related'.[12] It is in such traditional stories that the Matter of Britain found its roots. The myth of Mabon, perhaps once widespread, a story to be related as part of a seasonal ritual during the winter months, became merely the story of Mabon in later times. I write 'merely', but the hero-cycles which are told of semi-mortals like CuChullain, Fionn and others proved memorable in both oral and literary tradition. May we legitimately posit the existence of Mabon's archetype through a series of linked hero-stories?

The repertoire of a professional Celtic story teller including the learning of some 350 stories in which individual heroes appeared in definable story-cycles. Thus the story teller could relate the following tales about the hero's life: his conception, his youthful exploits, his adventures, his wooing of a maiden, his otherwordly voyaging, his hostings and raids; and finally, his woeful imprisonment, vision and lamentable death.[13] I propose to reconstruct here a similar hero-cycle applicable to Mabon's archetype, by juxtaposing stories of other heroes who share in some part of the Mabon mythos, or which they have inherited in the process of oral transmission. Such is the wealth of material scattered throughout both Celtic and Arthurian texts that such an experiment is possible. If Mabon represents x, the unknown factor, in this mythic equation, we must set something to work in his place and see what manner of revelation is given.

We are able to tell one story of Mabon's conception, or *compert*, as the Irish story-lists define it. For a Divine Child like Mabon we would expect to know of at least one otherworldly parent, and this is the case:

'In Denbighshire there is a parish which is called Llanferres, and there is a Rhyd y Gyfartha (Ford of Barking). In the old days, the hounds of the countryside used to come together to the side of that ford to bark, and nobody dared to go to find out what was there until Urien Rheged came. And when he came to the side of the ford he saw nothing there except a woman washing. And then the hounds ceased barking, and Urien seized the woman and had his will of her; and then she said: "God's blessing on the feet which brought thee here." "Why?" "Because I have been fated to wash here until I should conceive a son by a Christian. And I am the daughter to the King of Annwn, and come thou here at the end of the year and then thou shalt receive the boy." And so he came and he received there a boy and a girl; this is Owein, son of Urien, and Morfydd, daughter of Urien.'[14]

This Welsh story was preserved in oral tradition until the sixteenth century, and we may be sure that it tells the story of Mabon's conception, except, of course, that the story is told of Owain ap Urien, an historical character of the sixth century who was incorporated into Arthurian legend as Owain or Yvain, Arthur's nephew or cousin, according to some versions.

The fact that Owain's mother identifies herself here as a daughter of the King of Annwn is very significant, since a triad[15] speaks of the parentage of Owain and Morfudd from Urien and *Modron, daughter of Afallach*. Both the folk story and the triad obviously refer to the same tradition. Now, in Arthurian tradition, the wife of Urien is Morgan, Arthur's half-sister;[16] and Morgan is, in the earliest references,[17] the guardian of the realm of Avalon – Afallach being the original king of that paradisal island. Morgan is thus acting here in the role of Modron, and Owain in the role of Mabon.

Mabon's conception represents an intersection of linear time by paradisal dimension, for he is the child of earthly and otherworldly parents. Their meeting is the meeting of worlds, peoples, cultures brought into sudden alignment, and the divine child is born to mediate this set of encounters. The appearance of such a child, innocent and full of otherworldly knowledge, is the signal for a focalisation of opposing powers. All that does not wish to change, all that wishes to maintain the existing order and impose its will upon the world, gathers itself against Mabon, whose very existence represents a threat.

It is not possible to reconstruct a full hero-cycle for Mabon. Of his *indarba* or imprisonment we have already heard in the *Mabinogion*, noting that this is the most prominent feature of his mythos. That the *indarba* should occur so early in a hero's career is quite extraordinary, for the implication in *Culhwch* is that Mabon was stolen from his mother when he was a baby, though by the time of his liberation, he is grown to be a mighty hunter, capable of besting the fiercesome boar, Twrch Trwyth. This latter exploit represents Mabon's youthful deeds or *macgnimartha;* but perhaps Mabon's imprisonment is really of another order?

Within Celto-Arthurian tradition there are many instances of children being abducted, usually by otherworldly powers or in order to gain a special training. It is among stories of this kind that we can most authoratively see the half-covered trail of the Wondrous Youth, Mabon. There are two famous child abductions which bear obvious parallels with his myth, and a still more famous third: the abductions of Pryderi and Lancelot, and the obscure childhood of Arthur himself.

We learn that the abduction of Pryderi from his mother, Rhiannon, is caused by the enmity of Gwawl, an underworld noble who was once affianced to Rhiannon until Pwyll came to claim her. Gwawl was tricked into giving up his destined bride and humiliated by being put into a miraculous food-providing bag and beaten with sticks. For these blows he returns vengeance in one crushing attack: the abduction of Pryderi. It is not known how or where Pryderi is taken in the story; but, simultaneously, a British nobleman, Teyrnon, discovers that his own favourite mare has foaled. In previous years her foal had been stolen, and this night he keeps watch, for it is May-Eve, the time when the otherworldly powers are most free to operate. He sees a gigantic claw come through the stable window to steal the foal and strikes at it. The foal is dropped and Teyrnon rushes outside to pursue the attacker. Finding nothing there, he returns to discover a newly born child in his stable alongside the foal. He keeps the boy and names him Gwri Golden-Hair.

The boy is, of course, Pryderi. He is raised by Teyrnon and his wife while Rhiannon silently suffers the ignominy of standing at the horse block where she must tell her story to every visitor, offering to bear each into the hall on her back: her punishment for having eaten her own child, for so she stands accused. Gwri is, however, recognised and brought back to his parents and Rhiannon is released from her punishment. Her son is acclaimed by her with the saying:

'My anxiety is over.' And so he is named, losing his secret childhood name, Gwri, and becoming Pryderi or 'anxiety' instead.[18]

I have dealt with the many ramifications of this story in *Mabon*,[19] where the obvious comparisons between Mabon and Pryderi are paralleled. Here we note that Pryderi's 'imprisonment' is really a fostering. He is cared for by an earthly, astute guardian who raises him and gives him a name to protect him from the otherworldly powers which threaten his existence. Pryderi is not abducted and imprisoned by his family's enemy, Gwawl at this point, although this does happen in a later story when Pryderi is a man.[20]

Rhiannon is clearly shown to be a type of Modron in this story which best preserves the Passion of Modron. Like the unnamed mother of Urien's children, Rhiannon is likewise the daughter of a King of an otherworldly realm, Annwn, the Underworld. She is likewise fated to marry a mortal man and bear a famous son. The symbolic attributes of Modron are distinct in Celtic tradition: she often bears twins, she is associated with the Underworld, and is often represented by horses, dogs and blackbirds or ravens. She suffers the loss of her child and undergoes a passion in this period similar to that of Demeter for Persephone, abducted into the realm of Hades,[21] or makes a lengthy search for her son, like the Blessed Virgin who loses her Son in the temple.[22] Great burdens are set upon the shoulders of Modron: those who lift them are the helpers and companions of the Great Mother, and they have their place in the freeing of Mabon from his prison.

The suffering mother is again a feature of Lancelot's own abduction. Indeed, the beginning of Lancelot's story is called 'The Tale of the Queen of Many Sorrows', where it tells of Lancelot's father, Ban of Benoic, who dies suddenly from the shock of seeing his castle burned by his enemies. His wife, Elaine, leaves Lancelot – still a babe in arms – on the ground and rushes to assist her stricken husband, only to turn back and see her son being embraced by a maiden who takes him away with her. She is none other than the Lady of the Lake. She takes him with her to her lake-domain where he is kept safe from attack by his family's enemies. The Lady does not name him, but calls him 'the Fair Foundling' or 'the Rich Orphan'. She raises him to be a knight and later arms and names him herself. He is then sent back into the world to avenge his father and restore the lands which had been stolen by his enemies.[23]

If we follow an earlier story of Lancelot's abduction, *Lanzelet*,[24] a twelfth-century text which undoubtedly drew on Celtic traditions absent from the *Prose Lancelot*, we find that Lancelot is taken into the Otherworld for the sole purpose of releasing the Lake-Lady's son from enchantment. This son is called Mabuz, and he has been cursed with cowardice by an evil magician called Iweret. Lanzelet is raised by the Lake Lady to become an accomplished warrior – a late example of the Celtic tradition whereby boys were trained in war skills by women-warriors.[25] The Lake-Lady likewise arms and eventually names Lanzelet, although he remains nameless until he has accomplished her will, which is to kill the magician who cursed her son.

In this story, Lanzelet is almost a substitute for Mabuz. Mabuz himself is unable to move freely on his own behalf, for he is destined to live a strange existence within the Castle of Death – a prison in which he is trapped by the curse and a prison likewise for all knights who stray within its walls, for it renders them cowardly also. He is unable to make free use of his lands, realms analogous to the Lands of the Living in Celtic tradition,[26] for these are held by Iweret. When Lanzelet is released from his fostering, a fully trained knight, he starts to accomplish all that Mabuz would have done, had he been free. He kills Iweret and wins back Mabuz's lands, but for Mabuz there is no ultimate release, for his curse cannot be lifted. It is so that Mabuz's lands are awarded to Lanzelet who also marries Iweret's daughter. In this story, Lanzelet is clearly Mabuz's active 'twin' or substitute – they are, after all, foster-brothers. The author of the story has not fully comprehended the ancient tradition of Mabon's imprisonment but knows sufficient of the story to incorporate it in some manner. It is as though 'Mabon's prison' instead of being the 'place of Mabon's imprisonment' has become 'the prison administered by Mabuz'. Lanzelet accomplishes the *macgimartha* or *slugard* of the Mabon-cycle in this story.

What of the third abduction of which we spoke? Mabon is closely associated with Arthur, who, according to *Triad 52*, undergoes a mysterious imprisonment:

'And one (Prisoner) who was more exalted than the three of them was three nights in prison in Caer Oeth and Anoeth, and three nights imprisoned by Gwen Pendragon, and three nights in an enchanted prison under the Stone of Echymeint. This Exalted Prisoner was Arthur. And it was the same lad who released him from each of these three prisons – Goreu, son of Custennin, his cousin.'[27]

These references are encapsulations of stories which are lost to tradition, but which were clearly associated once with the disappearance and freeing of Mabon in Celtic imagination. There is a later tradition in which Arthur is 'lost'. He is conceived on Ygraine by Uther, who visits her in the shape of her husband, Gorlois: a transformation which is effected by Merlin, so that Uther is effectually a daemon or incubus.[28] Arthur is taken away after his birth by Merlin in order to be fostered by Sir Ector,[29] although his fostering in the land of Faery is spoken of by Layamon.[30] Arthur is thus hidden at the time of greatest danger to himself, during the interregnum between Uther's death and his own revelation as the rightful king who can draw the Sword from the Stone. The early part of Arthur's life parallels the Mabon archetype, but what of its latter end? Arthur is destined to weld Britain into a single country with himself as overlord. Nearly all his attempts to live a personal life are failures: he is at his strongest when he serves his country, who we can see as Sovereignty, the Goddess of the land, who represents Logres or Britain.[31] He does not die, precisely, but is wounded and borne away into Avalon to be healed by Morgen.[32]

Both the abductions of Lancelot and Arthur are really fosterings, times of withdrawal and preparation for great exploits. From these and the other examples of our Mabon archetypes we can see some part of the pattern coming clear. The manifestations of Mabon's archetype betray distinct features: the child is born of a mortal and an otherwordly parent. He is lost or abducted shortly after birth – usually because he is a threat to the established order, or because he is in danger from enemies. He is raised secretly, usually in an otherworldly environment, where he learns deep wisdom and the skills for his destined task. He is released from his obscurity or prison by a character bearing characteristics similar to or more mature than himself[33] and is so enabled to start a life-cycle which proves to be redemptive, not personal. At the end of his life he does not die, but it withdrawn into a state of spiritual life.

We will see the latter part of this pattern more clearly from one of the closest exemplars of the Mabon archetype – Merlin. Merlin is born of a virgin and a daemon.[34] As Merlin Emrys, he is abducted by Vortigern's men, who are seeking for a suitable sacrifice to help sustain Vortigern's tower, which keeps tumbling down. This tower is a figure of the state of Britain – in collapse under an unlawful, bloody and treacherous king. The perfect sacrifice, say Vortigern's druids, should be a boy whose father is unknown.[35] Merlin Emrys fits this description perfectly. However, since he is a type of Mabon, there is more to him than first appears. He is the innocent child who can refute philosophers and make clear the state of the country. He reveals the true cause of the tower's collapse as being the two dragons which are imprisoned under its foundations. He reveals to Vortigern the true state of Britain both now and in the future in a series of brilliant prophecies.[36] Here we see revealed another part of Mabon's cycle, his *fis* or vision, wherein his inner knowledge of creation reveals itself to men.

Merlin Emrys prophesies and then helps establish the reign of the Pendragons: firstly Uther, and then Arthur. He is really their forerunner. This is significant in relation to Mabon, since an early Welsh poem[37] speaks of Mabon as 'the servant of Uther Pendragon': a single reference which helps us link Merlin's function as prophet with Mabon's own lost function as releaser and enabler.

We note that Merlin does not have a personal life. His function is to serve Britain and to act as prophet and adviser to kings. When his task is done, he is withdrawn to the realm of his unknown father, the Otherworld. Geoffrey of Monmouth speaks of his house with many doors and windows through which he can observe the heavens.[38] Merlin does not die, but voluntarily retires from the realm of men into his Otherworldly abode from which he can still remain in contact with Logres and from where certain people, sensitive to Merlin's role, can faintly hear the 'the cri du Merlin'.[39]

Merlin's withdrawal from the world, like Mabon's imprisonment, has not always been perfectly understood by the later Arthurian romancers who have spoken of his entrapment by Nimuë, Vivienne or the Lady of the Lake.[40] Merlin's spiritual maturity is mistaken for senile infatuation, so that they tell of his revealing the method by which he can be trapped in his crystal tower, under his rock or in his thorn tree – those later representations of his place of retirement – to sinuous and treacherous damsels. These stories merely reveal the deterioration of the tradition. For in later stories Mabon similarly undergoes a diminution where, in Chrétien's *Erec*,[41] he becomes Mabonograin, a giant warrior, trapped within an enchanted garden where he is enslaved to a faery mistress whose domain he defends against all comers.

Both Merlin and Mabon's later commentators may stray from tradition, but they yet manage to retain aspects of older fragments which do not come down to us in any other way. From Merlin's story and from related tradition we can establish the archetypical Mabon death story or *aided* which appears nowhere else: the withdrawal of Merlin to his *esplumoir*.[42] Although there is one further example from late Arthurian tradition which has possibly inherited a vital part of Mabon's archetype: the character of Galahad.

The Arthurian tradition is exceedingly persistent. Whatever has been honoured, reverenced or sained by holy custom remains embedded within the Matter of Britain, becoming mythologically subsumed in the variant texts. Their unravelling is the work of many scholars. We have seen how Mabon's archetype did not totally fade from the tradition but appeared in strange guises. It should come as no surprise to find that it resides in the highest flowering of the Arthurian legends – the Quest for the Grail.

The original Grail winner is Peredur or Perceval;[43] in him we find many broad traces of Mabon's archetype, as I have shown in my study of the *Mabinogion*. Galahad appears much later in the French texts and has always seemed to me to be a foreign usurper of Peredur's role. However, Galahad inherits not only the characteristics of Mabon but also those of Lancelot, his father, who, as Arthur's best knight, is directly descended from the Celtic original 'freer of the cauldron', Llwch Lleminawg.[44]

Galahad is conceived by Elaine, the daughter of the Grail guardian, Pelles, at whose behest and with the connivance of Dame Brisen, she appears to Lancelot in the shape of Guinevere, the only woman Lancelot desires.[45] In this mysteriously un-Christian conception of the most Christian knight, we see the ancient archetypal pattern emerging. Elaine, like Uther in Arthur's conception, acts the part of fantasy-being, a succuba. Her son, Galahad, is brought up surrounded by women in a monastery, just as Lancelot is raised by the totally female population of the Lake-Lady. He is brought to court by a holy man after his obscure youth and undertakes the quest for the Grail. What most people consider to be Galahad's worst features – his seeming priggishness and ultra-holiness – are revealed to be the simplicity and innocence of a man living a redemptive, not a personal life. His one function – the reason why he was born – is to reveal the potentialities of the spirit and release them, in the shape of the Grail. When this is achieved, he is withdrawn from the earthly sphere at Sarras, the Grail city, where his companions seem to see him die; but we must look on his death as upon Merlin's withdrawal to another mode of life. Like Merlin, who is aided by his sister, Ganieda, to withdraw into his last retreat,[46] so Galahad is enabled to make this transition through the mediation of the holy maiden, Dindraine;[47] as indeed Arthur is enabled to pass into Avalon through the mediation of Morgen.[48]

Here we see Modron's part in Mabon's hero-cycle; in whatever guise she takes, Modron appears at both the beginning and the end of his cycle. For Mabon is a servant of Sovereignty, of the Goddess of the Land. His service is to the land, a redemptive, not a personal life. He represents the truth and justice of the Goddess, his mother, from whom he comes and to whom he returns. He is, in fact, Sovereignty's son, when he appears as Mabon the Divine Child. His enemies always strive to imprison or sacrifice him because he is incorruptible, pure and discerning, but the truth remains that he cannot be overcome unless he voluntarily commits himself into the hands of his enemies.

We have traced Mabon's unfolding life and career from conception to withdrawal; what is his true purpose within our native mythology?

Mabon stands at the nexus of a three fold tradition. As a Celtic deity he is the joy of the Otherworld, the God of Youth and Delight. As a proto-Christian archetype, he is a Liberator of the Light, the

Long-expected One who redeems the world. In non-religious, Arthurian tradition – which inherits elements of the two former ones –
Mabon appears again as the perfect knight, conceived strangely,
destined to free the waters of the wasteland and bring the Grail into
manifestation through his offices.

The reason why Mabon cannot be found by one person's effort,
nor from the testimony of one animal, is that he cannot be known
by one single part of creation: he is the sum of creation. He is the
Child of the Dawn, the First Born of the Mother. It is his task to
harp creation into existence and to be the Shepherd of the orders of
creations – birds, beasts and fish all answer to him. He exists from
the beginning and can be found – in archetypal terms – within the
terrestrial paradise. His mythos explicates this in other terms – he
is known to be imprisoned, hidden or lost, just as our own innocence
is lost. Whoever finds Mabon finds the primal source of truth and
integrity. His mother, Modron, is the land, the goddess who guards
the gates of death and living. An exchange takes place between them
which is at the heart of native mysteries.[49]

Modron, for the sake of the land, permits Mabon to become lost
to her. She enables his birth into the earthly realms by lying with a
mortal man; in this way Mabon has dual divine and human citizen-
ship. He is brought up secretly and taught all the skills which he will
need. He forgets his origins but he remembers these at his initiation
into manhood, when he enters the totemic tree of time where linear
time is intersected by the otherworldly dimension. At this point he
is given his earthly name, although he never ceases to be a Mabon.
His mother watches over his career and either in person, or in the
guise of messengers, encourages and helps him to fulful his mission,
which is to reconstruct the primal patterns of peace which exist
endlessly in paradise but which are lost in the earthly realms.

The accomplishment of this pattern takes many forms: Mabon
may appear as a warrior, hunting down whatever is corrupt; or as a
poet/seer whose prophetic utterances show pathways through confusion; or as a sacrificial king, who brings justice to a war-torn land.
He does not live a personal but a redemptive life. He upholds the
honour of his mother in the persons of other women who represent
her in the earthly realms, priestesses who mediate her influence and

power; he is also a guardian of his mother's rights where she functions as Sovereignty – the Goddess of the Land – by wielding justice, truth and discernment in the administration of the land. He may act as the forerunner or adviser of a king. He is not permitted to perform rites of healing in his own right or for his own benefit, although he may enable others to do so. His part is to establish the patterns of peace, but others have to wield them. When these patterns are established, he must withdraw from the earthly realms and return to the paradisal Otherworld, where he is restored to his first condition, as the Son of Modron, the keeper of creation.

This archetypal pattern of Mabon's inner function has been drawn only from native sources and traditions, but it is not hard to see why the essential core of Christianity grafted so easily onto the existing mythos of the British Isles. There is almost no join, for the two traditions – Celtic, or proto-Celtic mythos and Christian mythos – flow together in an organic way. Ways of worship may change, but stories never.

The cycle of Mabon does not have to be forced to parallel that of Christ: they are the same mythic pattern. A seventh-century Irish poem attests to an intrinsic understanding of the Mabon archetype where it speaks of the Blessed Trinity as:

> 'Threefold God, three noble united Persons,
> Wonderful sole King of Heaven, infant, holy warrior.'[50]

The horn which releases Mabon from his long imprisonment is blowing to assemble all peoples to a meeting place outside time to discover that the mediations of *all* traditions are valid, that they grow out of one another and will continue to do so.

The purpose of Mabon for our own time is the same as for all times: truth, justice and discernment are the heritage of all peoples; these are the means of healing the wounds of our earth and the pathways by which we may restore our lost innocence.

NOTES TO MABON, THE CELTIC DIVINE CHILD

1 *Mabon and the Mysteries of Britain,* C. Matthews, Arkana, 1987.
2 *Roman du Silence,* L. Thorpe in *Nottingham Medieval Studies* V, II. 2761–5, 1961.
3 Shrewsbury School MS vii, fol. 200.
4 *Pagan Celtic Britain,* A. Ross, Routledge & Kegan Paul, 1967.
5 *A Traveller's Guide to Celtic Britain,* A. Ross, Routledge & Kegan Paul, 1985.
6 *The Mabinogion* trans. Lady C. Guest, Ballantyne Press, 1910.
7 *Ancient Irish Tales,* T. P. Cross and C. H. Slover, Figgis, 1936.
8 *Mabinogion* op. cit.
9 The story of Tuan mac Carill and Fintan, famous reincarnated Irish sages, reveal a similar pattern. *Cf.* Cross and Slover op. cit.
10 *Trioedd Ynys Prydein* trans. Rachel Bromwich, University of Wales Press, 1961.
11 Ibid.
12 *Celtic Heritage,* Alwyn and Brinley Rees, Thames and Hudson, 1961.
13 These are all species of stories which recur in the professional Irish story-lists. They are known, respectively, in Irish as: *compert, macgimartha, echtra, tochmarc, immram, slugard, rain, indarba, fis* and *aided.*
14 *Trioedd Ynys Prydein* op. cit. p. 459. It is perhaps significant to note that the greeting which Urien receives from Afallach's daughter is the same as the five-fold blessing found in some native British pagan rituals. A corrupt form of this blessing was collected in the Cheshire district:

> 'Bledsian we thyn fote that habben brung thee in this weges [ways].
> Bledsian we thyn cneo [knee] that sceol cneolin unto that sacren awltar.
> Bledsian we thyn wame; withuten swilyke we willen nat by.
> Bledsian we thyn breost forman in belte and in strang [beauty and strength].
> Bledsian we thyn lippa that sceol spricka that sacren nama.'

15 *Trioedd Ynys Prydein* op. cit. p. 185, Triad 70.
16 *Le Morte dArthur,* Sir Thomas Malory, University Books, 1961.
17 *Vita Merlini* ed. and trans. J. J. Parry, University of Illinois Press, 1925. See also 38 below.
18 In most of the examples cited as archetypes of Mabon in this chapter, the hero, when a child, has a secret name which is replaced when he becomes adult; this usually happens at a juncture when he accomplishes his youthful exploits.
19 C. Matthews, op. cit. chapters 2, 4 and 9.
20 *Manawyddan, Son of Llyr* in *Mabinogion* op cit.
21 *The Homeric Hymns* trans. Apostos N. Athanassakis, John Hopkins University Press, 1976.
22 St Luke chap. 2 vv. 41–52.
23 *Sir Lancelot of the Lake,* L. A. Paton, George Routledge and Co., 1929.
24 *Lanzelet,* Ulrich von Zatzikhoven, K. G. T. Webster, Columbia University Press, 1951.
25 *Warriors of Arthur,* J. Matthews and B. Stewart, Blandford Press, 1987.
26 His lands are called the Fair Forest and are described in terms familiar to anyone who has read accounts of *Tir mBeo* as the terrestrial paradise.
27 *Trioedd Ynys Prydein,* op. cit., p. 140. In *Culhwch and Olwen* in the *Mabinogion* op. cit. there is a rare reference to Arthur's imprisonment when Glewlwyd, his porter, lists this as one of many adventures he has undergone with his king.
28 The daemon or incubus is of course a real otherworldly being, but Uther's assumption of another shape enables the conception of Arthur, who may be said to have an earthly mother and an otherworldly father.
29 *op cit.,* Malory, Book I, chap. 3.
30 *Arthurian Chronicles,* Wace and Layamon, trans. E. Mason, p. 177, Dent, 1962.

31 I have dealt with Arthur's relationship to Sovereignty in the second of my two-volume study of the *Mabinogion: Arthur and the Sovereignty of Britain – Goddess and Tradition in the Mabinogion*, Arkana, forthcoming 1989.
32 *Vita Merlini* op. cit. (See also 38 below.)
33 This part of Mabon's cycle I have identified as the Succession of the Pendragons cf. C. Matthews (1987).
34 Wace and Layamon, op. cit. p. 145.
35 C. Matthews (1989). In my commentary on *Lludd and Llefelys* I have shown the many parallels of this sacrificial role.
36 *The Prophetic Vision of Merlin*, R. J. Stewart, Arkana, 1986.
37 *The Romance of Arthur*, ed. J. J. Wilhelm and L. Z. Gross, p. 19, Garland Pub. Inc. 1984.
38 *The Mystic Life of Merlin*, R. J. Stewart, Arkana, 1986.
39 *Merlin*, ed. H. E. Wheatley, Early English Texts Soc., p. 692. 1869.
40 *Studies in the Fairy Mythology of Arthurian Romance*, L. A. Paton, Burt Franklin, 1960.
41 *Arthurian Romances*, Chrétien de Troyes, D. D. R. Owen, Dent, 1987.
42 Cf. John Matthews' essay, *Merlin's Esplumoir*, in this volume, p. 123.
43 *Mabinogion* op. cit. and Chrétien de Troyes op. cit.
44 *op. cit.*, C. Matthews, (1987), pp. 107–8, 156.
45 Malory, Book XI, chap. 2. I have examined the role of the dream-woman or succuba from her roots in the Sovereignty figures of Celtic tradition in *Arthur and the Sovereignty of Britain* op. cit.
46 *Vita Merlini* op. cit. and 38 above.
47 *Quest of the Holy Grail*, trans. P. Matarasso, Penguin, 1969.
48 *Vita Merlini* op. cit. and 38 above.
49 Op. cit. C. Matthews (1987), pp. 177–86.
50 *Irish Origin Legends and Genealogy*, Donnchadh Ó Corráin, in *History and Heroic Tale: A Symposium*, ed. T. Nyberg, Odense University Press, 1985.

Little Gwion

*A saga or monologue based upon the verses
Gwion's Adventure at the Grotto-aux-Fées and
Gwion's Return which have been recently
discovered and restored by Caitlín Matthews*

NOTE ON THE VERSES

'If Geoffrey of Monmouth, when he translated Tyssilio, had known the works of Taliesin and Llywarch Hen, he might have found in them abundance of historical passages that would have served better to enlarge and embellish that venerable and authentic history, then those legendary tales and incredible fictions he has adopted.

– Juvat integros accedere fontes.

But lest the purity of these genuine sources yet unexplored should be doubted, let it be remembered that the descendants of the Celts could never be brought to think with the Greeks and Romans on the subject of heroic Poetry, which was held in such reverence by that primitive nation and its posterity, that fable and invention (the essence of the classical *epopée*) were never suffered to make any part of it ... What in one country is called an heroic poem, and the grandest performance of human art, is despised in another as a fabulous empty song, calculated to please a vain and boastful people, who have no actions of their own virtue and courage to be recorded, but are constrained to have recourse to fictitious gods, fictitious heroes, fictitious battles, and such anachronisms as a grave British writer would have blushed to own. Historians who are acquainted only with the compositions of this character, may well regard Poetry with the contempt they have usually testified, as a vain art, that draws its materials more from fancy than nature, delights in fiction rather than truth. But widely different is the Poetry of the British Bards, which has ever been from the first of times the sacred repository of the actions of great men.'

Edward Jones (Iolo Morgannwg) *Musical and Poetical Relicks of the Welsh Bards*

It is possible that the discerning and well-read reader may in the ensuing verses find such recollection of his native lore as may render him speechless. Those persons who find the matter obscure are directed to the venerable Lady Charlotte Guest's valiant translation of *Hanes Taliesin* in the *Mabinogion*. It grieves the collector of these antique versus that men have doubted their authenticity. But let her assure all good British readers that the evil rumour which derives this precious relic of our most noble Poet's youth from a spurious tale concerning a Saxon infant, by name Albert, who so lacerated the ear of a lion, that the said kingly beast did swallow him up (deservedly so in the collector's opinion) is based on false report.

Gwion's Adventure in the Grotte-aux-Fées

1   There's a famous lake high up in Snowdon,
    That's noted for harping and song.
    And Mr and Mrs Morgannwg
    Went there with young Gwion, their son.

2   A bright little chap was young Gwion,
    He'd sung at Eisteddfods galore.
    When he'd finished Iolo's concerto
    The people would cry out for more.

3   They got to the top of the mountain
    And saw from druidical dome
    They'd arrived in the druids' off-season,
    And they'd have to go bloomin' well home.

4   'When I think of the waste!' cried out father,
    'Of the practice young Gwion has done.
    He might have stayed home and played englyns
    Like any young ordinary son.'

5   They'd started back home down the mountain
    When they sighted a sign on a pin.
    'The Grotte-aux-Fées' read the notice.
    Mother said, 'Must we pay to get in?'

6   A woman she stood at the entrance
    A-rattling her cash-till at Pa,
    She issued them tickets for fourpence
    And said, 'Nice day, have you come very far?'

7   She'd hair like the mould on Caerphilly,
     Her skin it was rough to the touch.
     Pa and Ma didn't make nothing of it,
     But you could tell they weren't liking it much.

8   But now that they'd paid for to enter,
     Pa and Ma they stepped forward with a will.
     Young Gwion he rushed in before them,
     Determined to show off his skill.

9   For a harp stood right there in the corner
     Its wires all rusty as tin.
     'Step up, come right in,' it sung sadly,
     'But beware, do try not to fall in.'

10   For there on the floor stood a cauldron
     All bubbling and brewing with smoke.
     Pa and Ma staggered back in amazement –
     Young Gwion he started to choke.

11   Said the woman, 'It's only my washing,
     No guests were expected today.
     Usually in the druids' off-season
     We lock up the Grotto-aux-Fées.'

12   'Since you're here though, look round and enjoy it,
     It's seldom folk visit me here.'
     Said Pa, 'And to think I spent fourpence,
     I'd have better laid down for good beer.'

13   'Take a bold front,' says mother,' 'and smile, love,
     We might not be enjoying it much,
     But young Gwion is mighty excited.
     Just look, love! – No son! Do not touch...'

14   Too late did young Gwion perceive it;
     He fell in the pot with a splosh,

'So sorry.' – Says mother, 'No matter!
I said that he needed a wash!'

15 Well Mother and Father were outraged,
They'd only paid out to look round;
They never expected to lose him.
Ma said they would stay 'til he was found.

16 'If it weren't for the expense,' cried out Father,
'I'd have waited' til Candlemas-come.
As it is I've a miner's convention
So we'll have to go bloomin'-well home.'

17 Said the fée: 'It 'twas to be expected,
If to heed their own parents' advice
Young boys were remiss and so careless
They were bound to be drowned in a trice.'

18 'But to leave that great cauldron untended
Was asking for trouble,' said Ma.
'If the boy cannot read that big notice,
He's scarce educated,' said Pa.

19 'Just think of the money we'll save then,
No harp-strings to buy for a start!
No lessons in rhyming, no ogham,
No music! Eh, mother, take heart!'

20 'Just think of the peace and the quiet –
A lodger we'll get for his room.
With money to spare we'll be rolling
– You can use his old harp for a loom.'

21 Says Ma, 'Now, it's not just the money,
I've a tidy bit now put away.
It's the principle that I object to.
How about recompense from this fée?'

22   Said Ceridwen, 'On your ticket, if you care to read it,
It says "To the Grotto-aux-Fées,
Admit one; washing taken on Fridays."
No mention of rinsing small boys.'

23   'However, seeing as you're so troubled,
I'll brew up my cauldron tonight.
And empty it first thing next May-eve
And see if young Gwion's in sight.

24   'Be warned, I'd not anticipated
That your boy would fall into the froth.
Stirred round for a year and well salted
He would make me a fine knowledge-broth.'

25   'Never mind your weird ways with the laundry –
It's Gwion she wants, not a soup.
Send him back well washed before May Day
Afore Mother here starts for to droop.'

26   And with that agreement they parted
And sadly from Snowdon they went.
His harp is put by in a cupboard
His room it is put up to rent.

27   But scarce had that year come right round when
There's news to the valleys of note:
They'd found young Gwion Morgannwg:
He'd come in this queer wicker boat.

28   Ma and Pa they rushed down to the river
To welcome their errant young son.
There were druids and men of distinction
All gathered to witness the fun.

29   'What's this?' cried out father in sorrow,
For no son could he see, clean and tall.

But a miserable fourpenny coracle
And in it – a baby – that's all.

30   'My son was well past thirteen summers' –
To the druids all gathered around.
'Have I raised up one son all for nothing
Just to raise up this baby they've found?'

31   Said a druid, 'There is no mistake here.
This note is quite clearly expressed:
"Please find one young Gwion Morgannwg,
His clothes they are still being pressed.

32   ' "We regret any great inconvenience,
But when he fell in with a splosh,
The management had no means of knowing
Young Gwion would shrink in the wash." '

33   'Great wisdom he must have acquired,'
Said the druids so sage and so wise:
'If swimming in cauldron's so clever,
How come he has shrunk to this size?'

34   Young Gwion looked out of his basket:
His face was as bright as a pin.
The druids cried out in amazement:
'Look brothers, it's Taliesin.'

35   Pa and Ma they were in consternation:
'A poet! That's all that we need!
Incarnations are all very well now,
But we've got a young mouth to feed.'

36   'Never fret, parents dear,' piped up Gwion.
'For my keep I will work very hard.
My income from one year's commissions
Will make me a lucrative bard!'

37   'Now like or lump it,' said father
     'Our Gwion's come home a might queer.
     Call it fate, or divine intervention,
     We've tumbled the luck of the weir!'

38   Now if your own infant's prodigious,
     And of his pronouncements you're bored.
     Just hurry along to the cauldron
     And slip our Ceridwen a word.

39   There's a Grotto-aux-Fées up near Snowdon
     What's doing a fair roaring trade:
     'Boys washed, dyed and pressed for a penny,
     Though not guaranteed not to fade!'

Caitlín Matthews

PART 3
MERLIN AND DOCTOR DEE

INTRODUCTION

by R. J. Stewart

The Elizabethan era was crammed with powerful romantic characters ... little wonder that it produced one of the great scientists and magicians of European history, Dr John Dee. In the following chapter Gareth Knight offers a short biography of Dee, with a number of astute comments on the philosopher's aptness to the reign of Elizabeth.

Dee is known to the modern reader through his curious magical experiments, usually set out for us in a popularised and totally trivialised form. We can often encounter dull nonsense about 'black magic' ... a charge which Dee could not totally avoid in his own time; on the other hand we have the rather pompous Victorian mystique attached to Dee by members of the 'Golden Dawn' who pilfered fragments of Dee's vast philosophical and metaphysical systems to use out of context in their rituals and disciplines.

Gareth Knight takes the sound historical attitude that Dee was a scientist, philosopher, and metaphysician. The remarkable achievements of Dee have been obscured by the ignorant popularity of his occult studies. There is more to Dee than either scientist or magician, however, for he may be seen as the Elizabethan Merlin. In this archetypical role, Dee becomes the seer of his time, the prophet associated (albeit uncertainly) with the throne, with matters of state, and with the lore of ancient British tradition.

There can be little doubt that Dee personally was familiar with traditions of Arthur and Merlin, and Gareth Knight reminds us that these were used deliberately as a foundation for some of Dee's political claims on behalf of the Crown. The conscious association did not necessarily generate the poetic similarity; a man does not become a type of Merlin merely by thinking of himself as such; our modern society produces enough would-be Merlins to prove this conclusively.

Dee, however, is one of a small, almost unnoticed group of men who span several centuries. We may include Merlin himself (if we allow him to be one or more historical persons in the fourth to the sixth centuries), Thomas Rhymer and Michael Scot in the thirteenth century, and the remarkable Robert Kirk of Aberfoyle in the seventeenth century. Such figures, historically proven and documented, also partake of the role of seer, magician, or explorer of other dimensions. Dee belongs to this group, and it might be reasonably expanded to contain a number of others.

There is no indication here that such a group is an 'order' or conscious formation; it is only found in retrospect by discovering men with similar otherworldly qualities in their lives. The common ground is not necessarily magic in the formal sense, but a relationship to beings and knowledge usually reserved within other dimensions. We might add that such men seem to be under the special guidance of a feminine archetype, fairy queen, or goddess. In the case of Thomas Rhymer we have a detailed account of his initiation in Fairyland and his love of the Queen; the primal relationship between Merlin and the goddess of the Land is discussed in detail elsewhere. (See Parts 1, 2, and 7.) Robert Kirk wrote a thorough and influential book on the Second Sight and Fairy lore. Dee appeared in the reign of the Faery Queen, Elizabeth I, and devoted much time and energy to perception of otherworlds. We can see a faint thread of tradition here, from the Dark Age Merlin, through the medieval seers and magicians, to Dee himself, and on to the work of Kirk in the reign of Charles II.

It is a tradition, not a conspiracy; a thread and not a web or plot; a harmonic connection and not a formal order or society. To attempt to explain or 'reveal' such connections as underground orders and magico-political movements is mere folly, or at worst blatant journalistic sensation. Having briefly considered these strange seers, let us now turn to Dee himself.

Figure 8   Reconstruction of contemporary portrait of John Dee

John Dee, the Elizabethan Merlin

by Gareth Knight

In the figure of Merlin we have a legendary embodiment of an archetype. An archetype of the white magician – the magus – one who plays a key role in laying down the patterns of destiny for the future at a critical phase in human history.

Sometimes the archetype may be seen to be at work in an historical context. An example of this is to be found in the figure of the 'Elizabethan Merlin', Dr John Dee.

When we look at Merlin, what do we see? An elusive figure, difficult to focus upon, shrouded in the mists of distant legend, yet a man of great prophetic wisdom, a man with strange knowledge, a man with strange powers; and above all we see a man with a love for the country where he lives, both the land and the people, that provides a golden thread for the whole of his life's work.

This man was once a miraculous youth, who thwarted the dark magic of the usurper Vortigern, and who helped restore the true Pendragon line upon the throne; who interpreted the portents of the stars to King Uther; who concerned himself with royal blood lines and brought about the conception of King Arthur; who saw to it that Guenevere had the Table Round as her wedding dowry; who supervised the founding of Stonehenge and by his arts arranged for the physical transportation of the stones; who oversaw and protected the young Arthur and brought him safely to the throne; who advised him on military strategy and political diplomacy; who wandered in many strange highways and by-ways; who consorted with feys and non-human spirits of the air, the water and the earth; who could see with prophetic vision into conditions of the future; who disappeared into obscurity when his work was done, when he had sown the ground, prepared the way.

And to do all of this, he had to be born into the right place at the right time, into a land that had a special task of destiny, at a time that was one of rebirth and crisis. For he had to show the way, to mark out the line of national destiny, to sow the seed ideas into the minds of the men and women of the time.

Such a time was that which saw the foundation of King Arthur and his Knights of the Round Table – wherever we choose to place it in historical perspective – and such a time also was that which saw the birth of Elizabethan England. Both times were crisis points in the destiny not only of the Isles of Britain but of the human race. Each time had its magical archetypal figure, the first in that of Merlin, the second in Dr John Dee.

John Dee was born in the right place at the right time and also in the right circumstances, in 1527, six years before the birth of Elizabeth, to a courtier of Henry VIII. He certainly did not have the guardian's control over Elizabeth's upbringing that Merlin had over Arthur, but circumstance saw to it that they had a close relationship, rather like a magical brother and sister – or at any rate cousins. John Dee's cousin was Blanche Parry, who was the infant Elizabeth's nurse, and he gave Elizabeth great comfort during the dangerous period of the reign of her half-brother and sister, Edward VI and Mary. For most of the time during their long lives the Queen admitted him to her court as a confidant or visited him herself at his house on the river.

Merlin had been almost a miraculous child. John Dee was hardly that, but he was certainly exceptionally bright. Born to Rowland Dee, chief carver and kitchen manager at the court of King Henry VIII, he went up to Cambridge at the age of fifteen and studied mathematics and Greek. These were very modern subjects at the time, almost outrageously so. Most learning, even of the Greek philosophers, was in Latin translation. Dee wanted to read them in the original. For this he studied under the great international humanist Erasmus, close friend of the recently martyred Sir Thomas More. Erasmus also encouraged him to travel, to break free of the cultural backwater that England at that time was.

His other very modern study was mathematics, and not only as an intellectual pursuit. He applied it to works of practical technology. In fact it was because of this that he was first accused of sorcery. At the age of nineteen he became a don, a fellow of the newly founded Trinity College, as under-Reader in Greek. Here he assisted in a college production of one of the plays of Aristophanes. For this production he designed a mechanical beetle which flew up from the stage with such verisimilitude that many were convinced it could only have been done by magic.

It is perhaps just as well that he did travel abroad. For it was very soon after that the ultra-Protestant commissioners of Edward VI burned mathematical books in the University of Oxford on the grounds that their diagrams were popish magic. But at this time John Dee was lecturing and studying on the continent, at the University of Louvain. Here he further showed the power of his intellect and personal charisma by a series of visiting lectures at the University of Paris, on mathematics, that were so popular that the halls were packed out and eager students hung from the very window frames to hear him. All this at the age of twenty-three.

His breadth of interests even extended to Oriental studies. It is recorded that for a time he became immersed in some Chinese didactic hexagrams – which sounds very much like what we know as the I Ching. He was also impressed by the contemporary magical treatises of Cornelius Agrippa. But in all his studies there shone through, as in all his life, a singular spiritual dedication. A motto that was close to his heart was: 'Nothing is useful, unless it is honest.' The study of magic in particular demands this high standard of personal integrity.

He returned to England in 1551, at the age of twenty-four, despite attractive offers to stay on the continent. One of his old college friends was now tutor to the young king, Edward VI. Dee found employment as tutor to the children of the Lord Protector, the Duke of Northumberland. These included Robert Dudley, later to become an early favourite of Queen Elizabeth as the Earl of Leicester, and his sister Mary, who was to become in after years the mother of Sir Philip Sidney. John Dee's interests continued to be wide ranging, including optics, astrology, medicine, the movements of the tides and of the stars, faith healing, and the propagation of the Gospel in America. He was always a devout Christian.

Within two years of his return, Edward, the boy king had died, and the Roman Catholic Mary came to the throne. John Dee was not prominent in the religious troubles of those times, but it was a

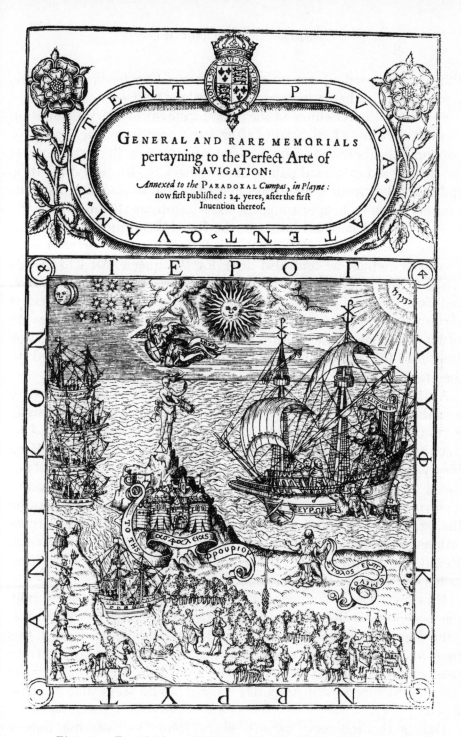

Figure 9 Frontispiece of John Dee's Perfect Arte of Navigation

difficult and perilous time for the princess Elizabeth, and by his association with her it became quite perilous for Dee.

Following the rebellion at the announcement of Mary's intention to marry Philip II of Spain, after two months in the Tower of London, Elizabeth was kept in semi-captivity in the gatehouse of the rotting old medieval palace at Woodstock. The decaying fabric and foul mists from the surrounding river marshes made this place a far cry from its former romantic associations as the hunting lodge where Henry II kept his mistress, the Fair Rosamund.

Here Dee wrote to Elizabeth, and to divert her drew up her horoscope, which he had also done for the queen. All Elizabeth's contacts were held to be under suspicion as a matter of course, and as a result of this correspondence Dee was falsely accused of performing enchantments against the queen's life, and of having struck blind one of the children of the government informer. He was flung into the Tower of London, closely interrogated and tried by the Star Chamber.

At this time people took astrology rather more seriously than they do today, and to cast the horoscope of someone so close to the throne, particularly in times of such controversy and difficulty, could be construed as an encouragement to insurrection. Indeed, when King Henry VIII had been on his deathbed, even his own doctors had not dared to forecaste his true condition, on pain of being accused of high treason. And during the following century, particularly during the ferment of the civil war, astrological tracts were used as revolutionary pamphlets. Some were called latter-day Prophecies of Merlin. One is still with us, though of less revolutionary proclivities, called *Old Moore's Almanac*.

However, Dee survived his interrogation and was eventually released, and in the course of time Elizabeth came to the throne. John Dee was sufficiently respected for his arcane wisdom at this time to be asked to draw up an astrological chart to appoint the most propitious time and day for the coronation. In the light of the subsequent success of Elizabeth's reign it would seem that he chose wisely.

During the following twenty years John Dee was not only a familiar figure at court; Elizabeth would think nothing of calling on him at his house in Mortlake whenever she passed. The palaces of Hampton Court and Richmond were close by. The Queen paid high honour to Dee, calling him her 'philosopher', 'my noble intelligencer', 'most faithful Dee' and 'my ubiquitous eyes'. He was also highly respected at court and enjoyed the confidence of Walsingham, Leicester, Sir Christopher Hatton, (Drake's patron), and even Lord Burleigh. Even so, the queen had to be cautious about advancing a suspected sorcerer to high office, and so he never received obvious financial patronage. Something of the ambivalent attitude that had to be shown towards him is revealed in his own note about Elizabeth's protection: 'Her Majestie promised unto me great security against any of her kingdom that would by reason of any of my rare studies and philosophical exercises unduly seek my overthrow.'

When Dee was taken ill in France, Elizabeth sent her own physicians to attend him. She also called for his aid when a wax image of her was found in Lincoln's Inn Fields with a dagger through its heart. In the presence of the Earl of Leicester and Mr Secretary Wilson he took steps to counteract the evil magic. His occult knowledge was also called upon by the queen when the whole court was alarmed at the appearance of the great comet of 1577.

As well as Elizabeth's own visits to his house, Lady Sidney was used as a go-between, and also Mrs Tomasin, the queen's dwarf, a lady who had a prodigious memory and so was well suited as a confidental messenger; but there were other callers as well, and in some ways more significant callers even than the queen. They were the great sea-going adventurers who made the Elizabethan age famous.

During his continental travels John Dee had become a close friend of Mercator, with whose name we are still familiar in Mercator's projection, which is a convention used in map making to depict a spherical world on a flat sheet of paper. In fact Dee had brought back with him two objects of great wonder and curiosity, a pair of Mercator's globes. They may be familiar to every schoolchild now, but they were not so then. What we are seeing is the first attempt of modern mankind to conceptualise the world as a physical celestial object. To do this man had to stand out from the world, so to speak, and view it as if an observer in space, from the background of the stars, almost indeed as if he were himself a star being. So these mathematical geographers of the time were, so to speak, the first modern 'planetary' men. This marked a great step forward in human self-consciousness, and John Dee was at the forefront.

And once again, with Dee, this was not just mere theoretical knowledge. He was inventor of a 'paradoxical compass' and made instituted manufacture of astronomical and navigational instruments in England. This was to become of supreme importance in making Britain a powerful maritime nation, able to challenge the Spanish and Portuguese monopoly of the New World and to fight off the great Armada. Indeed Dee also urged the building up of a strong navy, and deplored the burning down of the forests of England to make charcoal for the smelting of iron to export as cannon and small arms to England's potential enemies, at the same time causing a shortage of the vital oak that was needed to build our ships.

So we find men like Drake, Raleigh, Frobisher, Gilbert, Hawkins, making their way to Dee's house to learn how to navigate and where to sail. He had already, out of his own pocket, built up one of the most impressive private libraries of Europe. His pleas to form a national library, at the time of Mary, had fallen on deaf political ears, so he had put his money where his mouth was and started to do it himself.

Drake, of course, became the first sea captain personally to complete an actual voyage around the world, thus making the model globes of Dee and Mercator into a physical human reality. Planetary man had arrived, a step that possibly outweighs in importance our landing of a man on the moon.

Much of the immediate motivation for this travelling and adventuring was of course money. Men of the world willing to suffer incredible hardship and risk to their lives are unlikely to settle for less. Here again Dee was willing to risk not only his own venture capital but also his skin. He financed a voyage by Adrian Gilbert to try to discover a north-west passage to China, via Canada, and had it been successful might well have owned most of Canada north of the fiftieth parallel. Unfortunately Gilbert died in the attempt. Dee himself accompanied Frobisher on another voyage to Labrador.

It was, however, by no means easy money, nor even *only* a search for money. Apart from the quest for trade routes and for treasure there was also a struggle for domination of a new world. Spanish and Portuguese ships had discovered and exploited the West Indies and Middle and South America, and the Pope, as Christ's vicar on Earth, had granted exclusive rights to these two great Catholic powers, all newly discovered worlds to be divided between them. John Dee challenged this ruling by recourse to legendary history. He justified the right of England to settle colonies and trading posts on the North Atlantic seaboard of America, or Atlantis, as he chose to call it. He did this by publicising the legend of Madoc, the twelfth-century Welsh prince, who had not only discovered North America but settled there. There is indeed an evergreen legend in the United States of a tribe of white Indians, said to have been descended from the Welsh prince Madoc. They eventually suffered the fate of most Indian tribes in the great emigrations from Europe in the nineteenth century. Being white did not help them.

In the course of time, particularly under the initiative of Sir Walter Raleigh, the colony of Virginia was founded, named after the Virgin Queen. Even so, the first two settlements were wiped out by disease and famine. Success was not assured until the early years of the seventeenth century with the successful cultivation of tobacco as a cash crop. Other colonies followed – of persecuted Roman Catholics in Maryland, of persecuted Dissenters in New England. Whatever the rights and wrongs of it all, the trials and tribulations of civilisations on the move, the fact that English is the main language of the United States and Canada is largely due to the zeal and navigational knowledge of John Dee.

He was a great believer in empire. This is not a very respectable concept nowadays, in the aftermath of the European powers' land grabbing and exploitation of native peoples during the nineteenth and early twentieth centuries, culminating in two world wars by rival imperialist powers; but Dee was a believer in it before it happened. He could see it coming, willy-nilly, and he was determined that the conquest of the seas by the new navigational knowledge and skills should not result in a conquest of the world by a repressive spiritual and intellectual and physical power characterised by the Inquisition and the Conquistadores.

John Dee's conception of empire was a high one, and he quoted from Cicero in formulating the ideal of a 'whole and only one mystical city universal'. In the sense of world unity, be it under the aegis of the League of Nations or the United Nations, this is still something we have to achieve. It was as far off then as it seems to be now, but Dee saw any possibility of its realisation more likely under English than Spanish rule.

On the title page of his *General and Rare Memorials pertaining to the Perfect Art of Navigation*, an engraving shows Elizabeth seated at the helm of a ship of state bearing the name 'Europe', with the arms of England emblazoned on its rudder. Elizabeth stretches out her hand to an allegorical figure of Opportunity, who offers her a crown of laurel.

This was part of a general movement, in which Dee was prominent, which believed that, with the Protestant Elizabeth resuming religious authority, England was returning to an earlier, pre-Constantinian, ideal of an empire independent of Rome and the Pope. The assertion of Dee, Foxe and others was that, through the Celtic Church, England had received an earlier, purer form of Christianity, and kept it undefiled.

John Dee could see the age of imperialism coming. He also saw that if the way of life represented by all he held dear in England was to survive, then England had to become involved in the struggle – either challenge Spain and Protugal or go to the wall and betray the country's destiny.

So the reason for their being so much British Empire red on the maps of the world before the Second World War, was due in large part to John Dee; and perhaps of more lasting cultural importance, the English language becoming the principle medium of international communication was also largely due to him.

This is all the more remarkable when one considers what a comparative backwater England was at the beginning of his times. So backward was it that the calendar was ten days out from the rest of Europe. Encouraged by the queen, Dee strove to introduce the Gregorian calendar to England in 1582. His contemporaries, particularly the Anglican bishops (who saw it as a concession to Popery), did not want to know, and it was in fact not until 1752, one hundred and seventy years later, that his proposal was finally put into practice. Maybe this was just as well for him, because when it did occur there were riots in the streets with mobs indignantly demanding their ten days back. They felt that with the change of the calendar they had been deprived of ten days of life.

Dee found quite enough trouble with ignorant mobs as it was. His house and library were ransacked when he was on his extended European travels. However, the queen made him a grant of money to help to compensate for it, just as she had sent him forty angels in gold to help him entertain Albertus Laski, the envoy of the King of Poland, which led to his embarkation on his seven-year trip to middle Europe with Edward Kelley. Again, the reason for the looting was fear of magic and sorcery.

This has become the albatross that has been hung around John Dee's neck, started off by anti-Tudor propaganda, and compounded by the prejudice and ignorance of intervening materialist-minded centuries. He was, it should by now be realised, very far from the ignorant dupe of a fraudulent medium as has become the distorted image. The travesty is on a par with the tradition of Merlin being a sexually besotted old man englamoured with his own magic by one of the nymphets of the Lady of the Lake. In fact Merlin's disappearance into a cavern or a hawthorn tower is a profound poetic image of his merging with the land, in the way of a traditional priest king. It is a true marriage of life dynamics, an inter-polarity of heaven and earth in a most profound way.

Similarly Dee's allegedly obscure and ludicrous concourse with spirits was an attempt to make intelligent communications with a possibly superior race of beings. We assume it to be self-evident in our own time that man is the most superior creature upon the Earth. This belief would have seemed quite ludicrous to most people living anything more than a couple of hundred years ago. So maybe we are currently going through a temporary aberration of spiritual shortsightedness. Hitherto, communication with the heaven worlds was the prerogative of priests or elders of the tribe when mankind was more group conscious. In a time of the burgeoning of the individual spirit of man, and the individual responsibility of man, John Dee sought the right of any man, of any serious and spiritually

93

informed investigator, to make contact with the higher or the inner worlds – if such there be. He intended to find out.

His researches into what we nowadays tend to call the paranormal were most wide ranging. He was familiar with the technique of the pendulum and the dowsing rod. In fact he had sought a licence from Lord Burleigh, the Secretary of State of the time, to seek buried treasure by these means on his travels to Wales and the West Country.

These travels were partly to examine genealogical records to try to establish documentary proof of the lineage of the Tudor dynasty with the ancient Welsh aristocracy and possibly with King Arthur himself. The Tudors in fact had a somewhat embarrassingly weak claim to the throne by blood right.

Henry VII had gained the throne from the feuding houses of Lancaster and York by dispatching Richard III on Bosworth field, but his main claim by blood was through the second marriage of the widow of Henry V, French Katherine, to Owen Tudor, who was not much more than a jumped-up country gentleman. For this reason much was made by the Tudors of their Welsh ancestry and of the Arthurian tradition.

Indeed Henry VII called his eldest son Arthur, and but for the unfortunate early death of that youth England would have had another King Arthur instead of his younger brother, Henry VIII. This concern with ancient Welsh bloodlines was still going on in the time of Elizabeth, one of whose problems was that Mary, Queen of Scots, had, it could be argued, a more obvious right to the throne of England than herself. While he sought into the remote family history of the bloodlines of his sovereign, Dee also looked into his own, and proudly claimed descent from the old Welsh king Rhodri Mawr. If this was the case he was in fact related by blood, if somewhat distantly, to the queen.

However, of more moment to us are John Dee's researches while on this quest. These included what he considered to be a rediscovery of one of the secrets of the ancient Merlin, namely that Glastonbury and its surrounding earthworks formed a pattern that was an outline of certain constellations of the stars. This theory has had a considerable revival in our own day, with the help of ordnance survey

maps and aerial photography. How John Dee arrived at similar conclusions without the aid of these resources is open to conjec-
ture.

He was certainly very interested in all ancient earthworks, and
also in mines and caverns and medicinal springs, and related to
this was an interest in crystals and optics. He performed many
experiments with mirrors, some with quite startling results, and it
seems as if he may have come close to discovering the principle of
the hologram. It was said he could produce, by optical means, solid-
looking reflections in the air.

It is one of his optical devices that was the cause of a celebrated
visit of the queen to Mortlake one afternoon in March 1576, when
by an unhappy coincidence his first wife had been buried at the
church opposite that same morning. In view of his recent bereave-
ment Elizabeth declined to enter his house but asked that Dee fetch
out his magical glass for her. Accompanied by Leicester she alighted
at the church wall, and it is recorded that they found much diversion
from what may have been the images of a distorting mirror such as
are now commonplace at fairgrounds.

As those who have visited the Renaissance cabinets in the British
Museum will know, he had shew stones, or crystal balls, and also at
least one black mirror, made of polished obsidian of Mexican origin.
These, apart from any optical experiments, would have been for
psychic experimentation, although he seems never to have had any
great success with scrying (crystal-gazing) – perhaps being too intel-
lectually orientated.

He therefore had recourse to those who had, or claimed, a medium-
ist or clairvoyant gift, the most famous of whom was his close
colleague over a period of seven or eight years, Edward Kelley.

Kelley was no better than he should have been, and had certain
elements of the charlatan. However, it does appear that he did have
some very real gifts. Certainly he retained the interest of John Dee
over a long period, and it should be obvious from the record of his
life and attainments that John Dee was no fool. Much of this period
was also spent under the patronage of the King of Poland or the
Emperor Rudolf in Prague, and this part of the world was the centre
of spiritual alchemical expertise. Kelley in fact ended his life in

Bohemia, in somewhat unfortunate circumstances, it must be said. He apparently had made one extravagant claim too many and had been imprisoned, and fell to his death in trying to escape from a high window.

Dee returned to England. always his great love, despite lucrative offers, both early and late in life, to take up posts with foreign princes. All this despite rather parsimonious treatment he always received in England, but this seems true of the national character – we never treat our more brilliant prodigies too well. There were reasons for a brain drain then as now.

It was certainly not as a credulous and superstitious duffer that he was sought out as a teacher of Neo-Platonic wisdom by Sir Philip Sidney and his circle. He had, of course, been tutor to Philip Sidney's mother. It is this connection that was largely the cause of the intense revival of literary interest in Arthurian traditions in the late 1570s and '80 allied to the semi-deification of Elizabeth as Gloriana, or Astraea, the Virgin of the Stars. The longest lasting poetic monument has been Edmund Spenser's *Faerie Queen*, and the popular story of Sir Walter Raleigh laying his cloak before the queen for her to tread upon, which encapsulates, in a single image, a contemporary cult that was an English equivalent of romantic chivalry and courtly love. Allied to this is the mysterious School of Night, which was said to include such characters as diverse as Marlowe, Raleigh, Sidney, even Shakespeare and Bacon, which could perhaps give a line on some elements of authorship controversy!

Dee was thus promulgating an Hermetic philosophy to the courtly intellectuals of the time, that was widely accepted in such circles on the continent but which was as yet little known in England. The local applications of this philosophy Dee found in the legends of Glastonbury and the Arthurian tradition. The more general of these principles he expounded in his treatise on 'The Hieroglyphic Monad'.

It is interesting to speculate indeed on the possible influence of Dee upon the continental esoteric societies or mystical fraternities. His hieroglyphic monad appears in the margin of one of the famous Rosicrucian documents of the early seventeenth century, 'The Chymical Marriage of Christian Rosencreutz', and he was certainly treated with respect in the heartlands of the spiritual alchemical tradition, Poland and Bohemia.

Some have seen his extensive foreign travels and interest in magical alphabets, angelic languages and cypher as a cloak for secret-service activity. This may well be true. He certainly had close connections with Sir Francis Walsingham, the head of the Elizabethan secret service, Walsingham being the father of Sir Philip Sidney's wife. Many years later, in 1614, John Dee's eldest son Arthur received an appointment as physician to Charterhouse Hospital as, and I quote, 'a tribute . . . to my father's sagacity in giving timely warnings about the Armada'. There were those of course who assumed that he had received such intelligence through supernatural or diabolic means. This would be excellent pabulum for Spanish Catholic propaganda. However, at the time of the Armada Dee was in central Europe and probably gathering intelligence activity along with his other pursuits. He always was, after all, an intense patriot.

There is a rather bizarre element of synchronicity in all of this, as Robert Hooke, in an address to the Royal Society in 1689, revealed that John Dee's code number as a secret agent was 007. But whether he had a licence to kill, or preferred his cocktails shaken not stirred, is not recorded.

Dee's special talent as a gatherer of secret information is born witness to by some of Elizabeth's nick-names for him, for instance, 'my noble intelligencer' and 'my ubiquitous eyes'. His trips to Germany on her behalf, ostensibly to seek medical advice for her rheumatism and toothache, may also have sought intelligence of another kind. He had also warned her of the intrigues of the Duke of Norfolk regarding Mary, Queen of Scots, when other sources at court still thought him to be loyal. For this warning Elizabeth rewarded him with a gift of books.

The intelligence could work both ways, though, because it appears that Dee knew all about the supposedly secret visits of the Duc d'Alençon to Elizabeth, in one of her more controversial romantic affairs, he whom she affectionately nick-named her Frog, and saw as a defender of Belgian liberty against Spain.

'The Hieroglyphic Monad' aroused great interest at the time he published it, and he was invited to give special instruction in its mysteries to the queen. It is still in print, and is what might be called a private version of a universal glyph such as we find in the Tree of Life, or the Cube of Space, or the Enneagram. Much depends on the eye and the esoteric vision of the beholder. Dee himself reports that many 'universitie graduates of high degree, and other gentlemen, dispraised it because they understood it not'. However, he goes on, 'Her Majestie graciously defended my credit in my absence beyond the seas.' This absence was occasioned by his visit to the Emperor Maximilian II, to whom it was dedicated.

On his return to England Elizabeth desired him to read and explain it to her. The book was written in Latin which, however, was no handicap to the queen, who was an accomplished linguist. In anticipation of the difficulties of the learned in comprehending its contents Dee had inscribed on the frontispiece '*Qui non intelligit aut taceat, aut discat*': 'Who does not understand should either learn or be silent.'

Of his teaching of the principles of the hieroglyphic monad to her he records: 'She vouchsafed to account herself my schollar in my book ... and then in most heroicall and princely wise did comfort and encourage me in my studies philosophicall and mathematicall.' She states in a remark that he also recorded: 'Verilie, deare Doctor, you have contrived a moste economicall and ingeniouslie cunninge communication for your secrets.'

One is reminded of the strange device that Merlin set up, that is not often stressed in popular versions of the Arthurian stories, of a symbolic set of twelve statues of kings with lights to celebrate Arthur's achievement – to say nothing of the infinite meditational ramifications of the Round Table itself.

Both Merlin and Dee thus promulgated an extremely concise symbolic device encapsulating universal wisdom. They also both shared a marked decline. Maybe this is part of the archetype of the beneficent magician, the instigator of new patterns and processes. Once the spell has taken shape the instigator withdraws to let the outer-worldly humans get on with it. Thus did Merlin withdraw into a hidden tower after the fourth book of Malory's Arthurian legends.

In the latter years of Elizabeth's reign, things were no longer what they had been. It was rather like the Round Table just before the end. After the Grail Quest had been achieved, the Armada defeated, the globe circumnavigated, the King of Spain's beard singed – a sense of decline and anti-climax. Even Drake fell upon less than glorious times, until he disappeared into the sea at Nombre Dios Bay, as Merlin had disappeared into the Earth, or Arthur across the Lake, and become a focus for myth and legends of a possible return.

Dee was found a post in far-off Manchester, and Elizabeth played politics and bizarre games of love at court with the youthful Earl of Essex. New men had come to power. Old favourites were on the decline. Even Sir Walter Raleigh was in disgrace.

In 1603, the strange prophecy of Thomas the Rhymer came to pass:

> 'When Tweed and Powsail meet at Merlin's grave,
> England and Scotland one monarch shall have.'

In Merlindale in the border areas of Scotland, the Powsail broke its banks and converged with the Tweed, and England and Scotland came under one monarch, James I and VI, son of Mary, Queen of Scots, and representative of the Stuart line.

The new king had little time for alleged sorcerers. This was quite understandable. Throughout his troubled childhood there had been various attempts to assassinate him by occult means. Thus he had a personal interest in such matters, considered himself something of an expert on witchcraft and demonology, and wrote a book condemning them.

Of the old school, many were dead. Sir Philip Sidney had been killed in battle in Flanders. Drake was dead, and Sir Walter Raleigh confined in the Tower of London under the most ridiculous charges of being in league with the Spanish. He had for companionship Northumberland, known as the 'Wizard Earl'. (The title had passed from the Protestant Dudley family to the Catholic Percys.) Thus the new Northumberland, being a Percy and a Catholic, was there for suspected involvement in the Gunpowder plot. He had, however bribed the Constable of the Tower to allow him to fit up his quarters with alchemical retorts and stills.

Meanwhile Raleigh walked about, in his slightly old-fashioned-looking finery, forbidden to walk on the riverside ramparts, because when he did so all the sailors cheered him. The new king signified his disapproval of him in an oblique way, with a book on the evils of tobacco. In the longer term, in the light of modern medical science, the king has perhaps been proved right. Virginia tobacco, and dreams of empire, are today considered evils. All things, good and ill, have their season and pass.

It is said that here the Red Indian princess Pocahontas was brought to visit Raleigh and the 'Wizard Earl' by the latter's kinsman, George Percy, who had been one of the early colonists of the Virginia Company, before her tragic death at Gravesend on the eve of her return to her native land, and where her tomb remains to this day a focus for post-colonial trans-Atlantic accord.

What is it that causes this after-glow of inspiration that great men and women of vision leave behind? It is the same whether they be women of more than normal charisma, be they Guenevere, Morgan le Fay, Pocahontas, Elizabeth or Mary, Queen of Scots. They may be men of action and adventure such as Arthur, Lancelot, Raleigh or Drake, or wise men and prophets such as Merlin or Dee. What are we to make of them? They live on in the popular imagination. They are like constellations that give meaning to the mass of stars. They are like crystals, demonstrating coherent shape and form in basic natural matter.

Constellations, crystals, heroes. There is a link between all three. If we seek that connection, allow our imaginations to be lit up thereby, it is possible that our own lives will take on a structure of spiritual meaning too. Shakespeare speaks deeply of this, and to an extent even some of his works were influenced, each in their way, by both Elizabeth and Dee. Elizabeth had patronised him directly; the influence of Dee is more indirect.

The chronicler Holinshed, to whom Shakespeare went for some of his plots, had been a visitor to the library of Dee, and the strange island in *The Tempest* bears strong resemblance to Dee's description of Bermuda. Here, in his last play, Shakespeare portrayed a beneficent magus that some consider to have been modelled on John Dee. Dee himself was now dead and discredited. Whether this is so or not, Prospero describes the condition of himself and his companions of the magic isle in the famous words 'We are such stuff as dreams are made on.' Whether they be the imaginative characters of great dramatic art, or the legends and visions that develop about great men and women, be they Arthur or Merlin, Elizabeth or Dee, their influence is profound on all who aspire to follow after.

Their example is the golden key to an inheritance left us by our common ancestors, whereby is revealed the hidden stone within the Earth, known to the spiritual alchemists, of whom John Dee was a prime example and Merlin a legendary forerunner.

Arthur and Elizabeth were the crowned heads, legendary and historical, carrying the bloodline, under whose aegis these great instigators worked, whereby an alliance of inner wisdom and outer power and authority could come together to lay down a basic pattern for the next phase of human destiny.

PART 4
THE THREE CUPS

Introduction
by R. J. Stewart

The relationship between early Merlin texts, symbolism and tarot, has been examined briefly in Parts 1 and 2. In the story which follows, Rachel Pollack shows how imagery within tarot is used directly to generate a mythical tale; yet it is a tale that does not attune to any traditional body of lore. The traditional qualities come from the use of tarot images, and from her lucid story-telling style.

Thus we have the entertaining paradox of a totally modern original story which is also mythical and traditional; many fantasy writers struggle to achieve such stories, and often fail through over-contrivance. A true story has an organic quality to it that may be difficult to define in words, but which is always resonant and clear to the reader's or listener's imagination. This is where the tarot, in its primal and most potent function as story-telling images, has considerable value and potency.

Creating the story

by Rachel Pollack

The following story was composed specially for the 1987 Merlin Conference. Though Merlin does not appear in it, at least by name, and the characters are not those of the Arthurian legend, it does use certain themes from the Grail stories: the wasteland, silence, and of course, the cups. The term 'composed' is apt, for I originally told the story orally, using only a brief set of notes and improvising the details. The term also applies to the special manner in which the story came to life – with a set of Tarot cards, specifically the 'Solleone Tarot', conceived and painted by the Italian artist, Elisabetta Cassari.

Like a number of contemporary decks these cards emphasise action and story elements rather than occult symbolism. They also incline, in their imagery, to particular themes: oppression, feminism, sorcery, and violence. All these themes appear in 'The Three Cups'. At the same time, I did not bind myself to the meanings given by the artist for her cards, or even to the literal picture. For instance, the Wheel of Fortune in my story has a woman tied to it, not a man as in the picture; the sorceress appears in the desert rather than in a tower, and so on.

When I came to London for the Merlin Conference I brought along a selection of Cassari cards with me, having chosen them through the traditional means of shuffling the deck, cutting the cards, and then taking a particular pile. A day or two before the Conference I looked through the cards and found the Queen of Wands. The image of a woman running with a magic stick came into my mind, and with it the basic structure of the story. I then shuffled the cards I had with me and drew out several at random, including the Four of Cups, the Two of Wands, the Seven of Cups, and the Empress. I discarded the Seven of Cups and added the Moon, the Wheel and the Fool. As I developed the story I realised it would have to begin with the Three of Cups, a card I did not actually have with me. Though I knew the

Moon would be the last card, the end of the story did not come to me until a couple of hours before the story-telling session, a situation which made me rather nervous.

I would like to thank Caitlín and John Matthews for inviting me to the Merlin Conference, and Bob Stewart for giving me the opportunity to bring the story to a wider audience.

The Three Cups
by Rachel Pollack

There was once a woman named Catherine who lived with her mother and her husband and her daughter on a farm high in the hills. For many years they lived happily, working their land and caring for their animals. One day a man came walking up the hill to Catherine's house. It was hard to tell his age, for his face had become worn from sleeping outside. He wore a cloak made from the skins of various animals, and he carried a stick with a raven's head carved on the top. Catherine asked him what he wanted. He pointed to his mouth and shook his head. Then he made a motion as if drinking. No, Catherine told him, a drought had come to their country and they needed all their water for themselves. Again the man gestured. Catherine shook her head and went back to her work. With a sigh the man continued walking.

The summer passed and autumn came. The family began to prepare themselves for winter. One night Catherine dreamt that a voice called her to step outside. When she did so in her dream she saw that her land, and the hills around it had turned black, with all the animals dead and the plants withered. Everywhere she walked the broken sticks cut her feet. She woke up thirsty.

Two days later Catherine's mother went to the well to draw water for soup. When she brought up the bucket a snake lay coiled inside it. The snake slept until the woman tripped on a stone and water splashed on her feet. When she set down the bucket the snake bit her in the hand. By the next evening she was dead.

They buried her on a cold morning, after the first frost. They buried her on the far side of a hill so that when her spirit woke up and tried to go home she would lose the way and would have to begin her journey to the other world.

That night a storm came riding up from the lowlands. Catherine and her husband and her daughter locked the sheep inside their pens and took the goats and the chickens in the house. In the middle of the night the daughter thought she heard someone outside shouting for help. 'It's only the sheep,' her father told her, and she went back to bed. A little later she heard the noise again and got up and put on her boots. Lie down, her mother told her, it's only the storm woman. Once again she went back to bed. Just before dawn she got up again. 'It's Grandma,' she said. 'The wind has blown her back to us.' Her mother and father tried to grab her but she pushed them into the animals. The daughter let loose the latch and the door banged open. She forced her way into the wind, trying to call to her grandmother. A rock hit her and she fell back through the doorway. By the time her parents could close the door she was dead.

Catherine and her husband buried their daughter on the side of the hill, beside her grandmother. The whole way there and back Catherine refused to speak. When they returned she refused the wine her husband offered her in memory of their daughter. Instead, she lay down by the well and wouldn't get up.

For several days she stayed there. Finally her husband said to her, 'You and I are still alive. When you die then you can follow them. Now we have got to live.'

Catherine turned on her side to face him. 'This is no life,' she said. 'It were better you were created a tree than born a human being.' Her husband went outside and slammed the door.

All that night Catherine couldn't sleep, waiting for her husband to return. Long before dawn she got up, shaky on the legs she hadn't used in so many days. She went outside and shouted for her husband. No one answered but the animals. She walked as far from the house as she dared under the cloudy sky, calling his name. Finally she went back inside and sat down on the floor.

Shortly before morning she fell asleep. In her dream she kept telling herself she had to get up, go outside, find him. But no matter how hard she tried she couldn't open her eyes, couldn't get herself off the floor.

When she woke up she'd slept through the whole day. Ignoring the complaints of the animals she ran outside. The clouds had gone and a full moon silvered the earth. There, about forty feet from the house, stood a young tree, an oak still slender enough to bend slightly in the wind. Catherine walked up to it. Its roots snaked into the earth, its branches spread over her. As she looked up she saw the leaves filled with stars.

Catherine put her arms around the tree, she pressed herself against the bark, she stood back and shook it, hearing only indifference in the rattling leaves. She began to walk, half stumbling down the hill. For most of the night she walked, not caring if she tripped on roots or stones, or fell into the rough gorse.

Shortly before moonset Catherine saw her house and the tree. She realised she'd walked in a circle, going around the hill to the left. As she took a step towards home she heard laughter. Catherine turned to the side. Three women were there, dancing slowly in the last light of the moon. One was old, with a face all bone and line, another was young, with soft skin and long hair that swung heavily behind her. The third woman danced with her back to Catherine.

As Catherine watched, the dance slowed and then they all turned to her. Even the one in the middle turned, though her face remained hidden by the others. They were all holding cups, Catherine saw, silver cups with some dark wine that splashed onto the ground. Each of them raised her cup, and all nodded to Catherine.

'No,' Catherine said. She stepped back. 'I know who you are and I will not drink with you.' She ran, hearing behind her the rhythm of their dancing feet.

When she reached her house she learned against the door, breathless. The moon had gone. In the darkness she couldn't see if the women were still there. With a grimace of pain Catherine entered her home. Everything lay silent and dark. Ashes and half-burned pieces of wood cluttered the hearth and the space in front of it. She sat down on a chair she'd made years ago, when she was pregnant. No more children, she thought. No more voices. She got up and cleared away the ashes.

She went out behind the house to the open shed containing the wood pile. There on top lay a thick branch, more like a club than most of the neatly chopped logs stacked for the winter. She picked it up by its narrow end, held it in front of her. The bark felt fresh, as if someone had just torn it from the tree. She dropped it back onto the pile – or tried to. The branch wouldn't leave her hand.

When she grabbed it with the other hand to pull it free that one stuck as well. Frightened, Catherine tried to shake it loose.

Instead, the branch began to move through the air. Slowly at first, then faster, it travelled all by itself above the ground, forcing Catherine to run with it if she didn't want it dragging her along the stones and dirt. For hours it carried her, moving so fast Catherine couldn't understand how she could keep up with it. It carried her over the nearby hills, then past strange towns and deep into woods she'd never seen. The day came and passed. Running under the moon, Catherine thought she heard the three women, their rhythmic stamping, the splash of their wine. Then the stick carried her away, and all she could hear was the wind.

She was running east, she realised, for in front of her the sky began to lighten. She could see a city. It looked half in ruins, with broken buildings, and only a few lights far apart. Somewhere she heard a bell.

Exhausted, Catherine knew she was falling asleep. She hoped she wouldn't break her legs or cut them too badly when the stick dragged her behind it. But there was nothing she could do. She closed her eyes. Her feet kept moving. She fell asleep.

When Catherine woke up she was lying in a land she'd never seen, flat in all directions, hard yellow dirt with here and there huge brown rocks streaked with red, sitting on the ground as if they'd fallen from the sky. It was summer here, or maybe it was warm the whole year round. Though the sun was still low in the sky Catherine was sticky with sweat. The stick was gone. Her hands and feet stung from the wind and sun in her raw bruises. As she looked around her, she saw, about thirty yards away, a pool of water. Like someone slapping her, thirst made her gasp. She'd never realised she could so long for water. Hardly able to stand, she half walked, half crawled towards the pool.

She was almost there when she saw a strange creature, a fish, it looked like, with a bird's wings. No larger than her hand it lay there, its wings fluttering uselessly, its scales flickering in the sun. A green tongue, swollen and spotted, stuck out from the mouth. The eyes rolled towards her.

Catherine knew that if she detoured she would never have the strength to push herself to the water. But if she didn't help the winged fish she was sure it would die. She took another step towards the pool. But then she thought of her family, and with a groan turned to the left. She picked up the fish and threw it into the water.

Lying exhausted in the dirt she watched it splash and turn about, flapping its wings. It began to grow, becoming the size of her foot, then larger. As it grew it absorbed the water, until at last, when it lifted into the air, the size of a goose, the ground underneath it lay as baked as everywhere around it. Catherine hit a weak fist against the dirt. And yet, her thirst seemed to dwindle.

Looking up she watched the bird circle higher and higher until it vanished into the sun. For a long time it was gone and then Catherine saw it return, a dot on the edge of the sun, a flash spiralling down. As the bird reached her, Catherine discovered herself stronger. She could sit up now, could smile as she saw the green scales beneath the brown wings. She stretched out her arm and the bird settled onto her wrist. It spoke to her – a series of low whistles – and to her astonishment, she could understand what it was saying. It told her that a sorceress ruled this land, a red evil in the shape of a woman, a blood drinker who had broken the cities and drained the life from the earth. Catherine shook with fear. And then the bird asked her name.

Catherine opened her mouth – and stopped. Her name – why couldn't she remember her name? She tried to concentrate, it was so simple. Empty. And when she tried to say, 'I don't remember,' that too wouldn't come. With the loss of her name she could no longer speak. She could only watch as the bird let go of her wrist and flew away.

Holding the top of her dress over her head to protect her from the sun, Catherine sat until nightfall. With the darkness came the cold, the land cracking from the change as if it would break open. Catherine was about to go searching for people or water when a wavy red line appeared on the horizon. The line became longer, thicker, turning into a swirling column of fire. Catherine sat back down on the dirt. She tore her clothes so the raggedness would look rough, like stone. Then she bent over, with her legs underneath her and her arms over her head, which she turned to the side so she could see.

Before her, the swirling fire slowed until it became a woman spinning around with her red dress half clinging to her, half flapping in the night. Finally she stopped and stood with her arms folded across her chest, her head tilted slightly back. She took no notice of Catherine, only stood there, gently sniffing, like an animal searching the wind.

Behind her Catherine heard a shout, and then a man strode towards the sorceress. He wore rough clothes and no shoes, but he carried a sword. Catherine saw letters or pictures etched into the blade. 'Malignant One,' he said, 'this is the time of your death.' The sorceress held open her dress. The starlight seemed to gather round her breasts, while between her legs there was only shadow. She bowed her head. In a voice slowed by suffering she said, 'I have waited so long for you.' The man hesitated. Without thought he lowered his sword. The woman leapt at him. Catherine saw a flash of white as the sorceress bit the man in the neck. He grunted and sank to the ground. With a black cup from her dress the sorceress collected the blood. When the cup had filled, the man lay dead. The sorceress lifted the cup before her face. Her mouth moved slowly in a silent incantation.

Before the sorceress could finish her spell there came a great noise: drums, stamping feet, shouts, the clank of armour, a high-pitched trilling. The sorceress pressed the cup beneath her breasts. She spun around once and in her place there stood a tree, dead, with grey bark and no leaves.

A parade of people came marching across the desert. Led by two women banging metal plates with wooden sticks, they included a man in black armour and a masked woman shouting out a list of names. When they came upon the dead man lying beside his sword they began to wail or scream. A woman threw herself on the body, spreading over it as if she'd protect it from the birds.

Catherine stood up, wanting to go to the woman, to help her. As soon as she moved the others rushed round her, shrieking and grabbing hold of her, pulling her arms and kicking her. The sorceress had put a spell on her, Catherine realised. When they looked at her they saw the creature they hated most in all the world.

Catherine tried to tell them the sorceress had tricked them.

Nothing came out. She shook loose an arm and pointed at the tree. They only grabbed her again. They tied her arms and legs and lifted her above their heads. With great shouts and banging of drums they carried her through the night.

In the morning they came to the top of a cliff where a long row of women sat on wooden benches. They wore white dresses, the colour of sorrow, while they'd wound their arms with red ribbon, in memory of their dead children. Beyond them, at the edge of the cliff, with the first splash of sunlight lighting up his body, stood a bald man, naked except for a kind of leather skirt wrapped around the lower half of his body. His face and shoulders and the backs of his hands were scarred with deep lines cut into the skin. He stood casually. His right hand held an axe handle, with the blade resting on the ground.

When her captors had set Catherine on the ground, the rows of women stood up. 'This is the Council of Mothers,' a woman told Catherine. 'They have come here every morning, praying the sun to deliver them this moment.' One by one the women stretched out their ribboned arms to point at Catherine and accuse her of hideous crimes, of cannibalism, of tearing apart children or smashing their heads against rocks. Catherine wanted to scream, tell them it was not her, tell them the Malignant One hid in the desert, tell them she had lost her own daughter. Her throat remained locked. She prayed to the Sun, the Earth, to her dead mother to please give her back her name and her voice. Nothing came.

One by one the mothers came forward and spat at Catherine's feet. Then the others took her arms and dragged her to the executioners. As they bent her down to place her head on a block of stone by the cliff's edge, Catherine saw, in the midst of her terror, a dark spot spiralling out from the sun.

The executioner took his axe in both hands. He spoke a prayer of protection against the spirit which would fly out from the neck. Catherine struggled to get loose, but people on either side pinned her arms and legs to the ground. The executioner swung his blade high into the air.

The winged fish flew into his face. He stepped back, and at the same time dropped his axe. It fell behind him over the side of the cliff. Catherine heard a clang as it bounced against rock, and then a loud splash. The bird circled above her and flew away.

The executioner kneeled down and covered his scars with dirt. Everyone else began shouting and pointing at Catherine. Some claimed she must be innocent. Others insisted she had summoned an Elemental. Still others offered her a chance to defend herself. She pointed to her mouth to indicate she couldn't speak, she tried using her arms to say they must return to the desert. The accusers said she was casting a spell and held her arms behind her.

'Give her to the guardians,' they said. 'Let the guardians decide.' They led Catherine down the hill to the river. In the water, attached to a stone pillar, a wooden wheel turned. Around the rim, carvings, some just a face, others whole figures, stood out from the wood. Catherine saw animals, humans with bulging bellies and sharp teeth, a radiant child with outstretched arms. The river came a third of the way up the wheel, so that as it turned each of the carvings passed underwater to come out again into the light.

The people stopped the wheel and tied Catherine to the spokes. When they started it moving again, very slowly, her head came under the water with every turn. Each time she held her mouth shut. When she rose to the top, gasping for breath, the sun burned her. She became dizzy, and she knew that if she didn't drown she would die from the heat. 'Help me,' she thought, 'please help me.'

On the next turn down she once again closed her mouth. But now the winged fish came diving into the river. It swam at her face and she gasped in surprise. Water filled her mouth. It was sweet, soothing. She swallowed. And remembered her name. 'I am Catherine,' she shouted, as soon as the wheel raised her up again. 'The murderer hides in the desert. Let me take you there.'

The people stared at her. Instead of the demon they saw a ragged woman. They untied her and soon Catherine led them back to the dead tree. She reached between the branches and there stood the black cup, still filled with blood. Telling everyone to stand away Catherine threw the blood at the tree.

The moment it changed back to the sorceress the people leapt on her. They stabbed her in the heart, they crushed her face with a rock, they tore her to pieces. Rage had driven their souls out from their faces when Catherine stamped her feet and called to them to stop. They turned to her. 'Take the pieces,' she told them. 'Bury them in all the dead places. Ask the Mother of Life for mercy and help.'

The people did as she had said, drawing a guardian sign in the dirt wherever they had planted a piece of their enemy. Water came out of the Earth, and then plants, even small trees, and soon they heard the night sounds of animals, born, like the first beasts, out of the darkness.

Catherine stayed with the people for several months. But when she saw the crops growing and many of the women pregnant, she began to miss her own land. One night she went out after everyone had fallen asleep. She looked up at the full Moon. 'Help me,' she said to the face looking down at her. 'I want to go home.'

She heard a flutter and felt a wet breeze. With a smile she turned to the winged fish. As she watched, the scales fell off, the wings became white, and soon a giant swan was spreading its wings and nodding its head. She climbed on its back and a moment later they rose into the air.

Through the night they flew, with the Moon lighting the air. Tired, Catherine laid her head on the swan's back. Just before she closed her eyes she saw, far below, the three dancing women raising their silver cups.

When Catherine woke up she was lying on the ground in front of her own house. The animals, deserted for so many months, grazed or walked about, contented, as if someone had cared for them while Catherine was gone. She walked inside and there, on the table, stood a gold cup filled with wine. Catherine drank half the wine. A sweetness poured over her heart. She began to cry, letting the tears slide off her face into the cup. When it was full she took it outside.

The tree was there, heavy with leaves despite the winter that was just passing. Catherine poured the wine down the trunk. From inside the tree her husband walked towards her. He moved slowly, lowering upraised arms, turning his head side to side. Catherine took his hands and he smiled. Together they sat under the tree, holding each other while spring stirred the land beneath them back into life.

PART 5
MERLIN'S ESPLUMOIR

Introduction
by R. J. Stewart

In the following chapter John Matthews has touched upon two major aspects of Merlin legends, and of tradition in general. The most specific is that of the relationship between Jewish and European legend during the Middle Ages, a relationship exemplified by several motifs and themes within the Merlin texts.

In the *Vita Merlini*, for example, we find themes from Talmudic tradition, and from widespread folk tales found as far afield as Northern India. This poses the interesting question of sources for such tales, and, as John Matthews observes, exchanges of cultural lore undoubtedly occurred during the Middle Ages. There is no suggestion here of a 'diffusionist' theory, which might imply that Merlin stories travelled from the Far or Middle East, gradually becoming Westernised *en route:* such suggestions are merely a type of crude reductionism with a severely limited linear conception of human development and culture.

What actually happens is far more wonderful and significant than any linear travelling or migratory pattern: similar themes, tales, archetypes and mystical realisations concerning inner truth all share a symbolic language. In simpler terms, people all over the world dream the same dreams, share certain key images and tales, no matter how different their politics, formal religion and local practices or culture may be. This does not imply, by the way, a kind of cosy universalism, for the intense differences between cultures and traditions often outweigh the shared aspects; but as we move into the deeper levels of poetic or spiritual symbolism, we find many shared images.

It is on this level that we find important connections between Merlin, Metatron, Elijah, Enoch and Messianic tradition not necessarily connected in any way to the orthodox Christian concept of Christ as the Messiah. Indeed, Merlin as a saviour or universal prophetic master, seems to attune more strongly to Jewish mystical tradition, not because of any direct migratory relationship in the tales, but as a curious side-effect of political restrictions imposed by Christianity, which effectively debarred such traditions as active means of spiritual education. In other words, the traditions were always present, but seem in retrospect to relate to other cultures through the enforced absence of certain poetical or sacred themes from state religion.

In most cultures the prophet, sacred ruler, or hidden master, is a recognised figure within spiritual tradition and personal inner development; in medieval Europe, however, writers who preserved ancient traditional themes were obliged to edit carefully material already heavily altered through political religious influence. We are, in short, fortunate that Merlin texts survived at all, as at one time it seemed very likely that Merlin was being set up as a potential 'antiChrist' ... a terrible negative concept far removed from the primal innocence and beauty of the Child of Light from which he seems to have grown.

The second important aspect brought forward by John Matthews is that of the deeper levels of the 'Hidden Master' tradition; we might call these the metaphysical levels, in which we detect implications of the relationship between human awareness and the greater or macrocosmic divine consciousness. Traditions of this sort are enduring and deep, and very different indeed from the trivial notions of superhuman masters that abound in fashionable 'New Age' publications.

There is an important difference between commercialised fictitious personae sold to meet our collective emotional need for reassurance, and the perennial traditions of certain masters or teachers who remain upon inner or conceptual dimensions of consciousness. These beings, found worldwide in mystical practice, are a far cry from cosy helpers or extra-terrestrial last-minute saviours. They are often stern, terrifying and utterly uncompromising in their dealings with mortals, mainly because they too were once human and know our failings only too well.

Merlin's Esplumoir

by John Matthews

It has become customary to view the end of Merlin's career in a certain light: as an ageing magician captivated by a young woman. In this scenario Merlin is beguiled into giving away his greatest secrets in return for sexual favours; once the temptress – whose name may be Nimuë, Niniane or Vivienne – has succeeded in extracting this knowledge she at once uses it to imprison her aged lover, sometimes under a great rock, sometimes within a hawthorn bush, sometimes in a glass tower. From here he is said to utter elusive prophecies or gnomic sayings, while in some versions the 'Perron de Merlin', Merlin's Stone, becomes a starting point for adventure, to which those in search of the strange or the mysterious resort, to await events or instruction.

Such is the story which Malory, for instance, gives us in the *Morte d'Arthur*, Book IV, Chap. 1.

'Merlin fell in a dotage on the damosel that King Pellinore brought to court, and she was one of the damosels of the lake, called Nimue. But Merlin would let her have no rest, but always he would be with her. And ever she made Merlin good cheer till she learned of him all manner thing that she desired; and he was assotted on her, that he might not be from her ... And so, soon after, the lady and Merlin departed ... and always Merlin lay about the lady to have her maidenhead, and she was ever passing weary of him, for she was afeared of him because he was a devil's son, and she could not be rid of him by no means. And so on a time it happed that Merlin showed her in a rock whereat was a great wonder, and wrought by enchantment, that went under a great stone. So by her subtle working she made Merlin to go under that stone to let her wit of the marvels there; but she wrought so there for him that he came never out for all the craft he could do. And so she departed and left Merlin.'

Tennyson, four hundred years on, reinforced this in Victorian dress in his poem 'Merlin and Vivien' from *The Idylls of the King*; but there is another version. In this story, which we find in Geoffrey of

Monmouth's *Vita Merlini*,[1] the *Didot Perceval*[2] and various other texts, Merlin has reached a great age, or a particular stage of spiritual development, and decides to retire from the world *of his own accord*. He is, sometimes, still accompanied by a female companion, though, as in the *Vita*, it is more likely to be his sister than his lover, and the place of retirement may still be a tower, an island or a cave, but these are places of Merlin's own choosing or even construction.

The question is: which of these two versions is the right one, if indeed there is a right one; and which motivation – lust or continued growth – should we believe? To answer this we have to ask another question: Why should Merlin withdraw from the world? I have already suggested one answer: that he sought further knowledge or the opportunity to grow. Fortunately there are several other figures, though from a different tradition, each of whom shares some of Merlin's attributes as prophet, mystic, and seer, and has a specific reason for withdrawing. Consideration of these figures may help to clarify matters.

The figures in question are generally known by the term 'hidden' or 'inner' kings, beings who have responsibility for a particular aspect of tradition or teaching and who continue to administer this even after they have withdrawn from active participation in the events of the world, although they are not actually dead. Among the most notable are Melchizadek, Enoch, Elijah and, I believe, Merlin himself.

Despite their many differences these figures share certain important aspects. They are all mysterious, shadowy beings, who appear at a time of crucial import, and who seem to have neither an orthodox beginning nor end to their lives. Finally, they each withdraw or disappear, leaving conflicting accounts of their actual existence, function or allegiance.

Melchizadek, we may remember, was 'without beginning or end'[3], while Enoch 'walked with God and was not'[4] but beyond this seems to have no point of origin. He is first mentioned, in Jewish traditional sources – significantly as we shall see – as living in a hidden place, from which he watches and records the deeds of mankind and holds occasional converse with God. Later he is represented as a king over men who ruled for more than two hundred years before being summoned by God to rule over the angelic hosts.

To this rather sparse account we can add, from various other sources, that Enoch visited heaven often while still in the flesh, and that he was instructed by the archangel Michael in all things, after which he wrote some 366 books, which may well remind us of the 333 prophetic books of Merlin ...

When translated to heaven Enoch had bestowed upon him 'extraordinary wisdom, sagacity, judgement, knowledge, learning, compassion, love, kindness, grace, humility, strength, power, might, splendour, beauty, shapeliness and all other excellent qualities', and received besides 'many thousand blessings from God, and his height and breadth became equal to the height and breadth of the world, and thirty-six wings were attached to his body to the right and to the left, each as large as the world, and three hundred and sixty-five thousand eyes were bestowed upon him, each as brilliant as the sun ...'[5] The description continues for several more paragraphs, outlining a truly cosmic figure. At the end it is revealed that Enoch – whose name, not surprisingly perhaps, means 'the enlightened one' – received a new name. As the text puts it:

> 'A magnificent throne was erected for him beside the gates of the seventh celestial palace, and a herald proclaimed throughout heaven concerning him, who was henceforth to be called Metatron. God declares: "I have appointed my servant Metatron as prince and chief over all other princes in my realm ... whatever angel has a request to refer to me, shall appear before Metatron, and what he will command at my bidding, ye must observe and do, for the Prince of Wisdom and the Prince of Understanding are at his service, and they will reveal unto him the science of the celestials and the terrestrials, and knowledge of the present order of the world, and the knowledge of the future order of the world. Furthermore have I made him guardian of the treasures of the palace of heaven, Arabot, and of the treasures of life that are in the highest heavens."[6]

Enoch has thus become a Lord of Hosts and a guardian of the Treasures of Life in heaven. More interestingly perhaps he is also said to have assumed the position left vacant by the fall of Lucifer.[7] He is thus balancing out the uneven ranks of the angelic host, and perhaps it is not stretching the analogy too far to see here an echo of the place left empty at the Round Table, which will one day be filled by the destined champion of the Grail. I think also that in the description of the revelation of the sciences celestial and terrestrial, the knowledges of present and future, we have another analogy of the knowledge and wisdom of Merlin, derived from within his observatory with its 70 doors and windows.[8]

Many ages after the withdrawal of Enoch another figure appears to represent the mysterious hierarchy of the withdrawn kings. This is Elijah, who even in Biblical sources comes across as a rather contankerous, argumentative character, not at all above telling God how things ought to be done. The story is told that when the time came for him to ascend to heaven, the Angel of Death was reluctant to admit him. Elijah argued so violently before the gates of heaven that God Himself was forced to intervene and gave permission for a wrestling match between Elijah and the Angel. Elijah was victorious and now sits with Enoch and Melchizadek, like them recording the deeds of mankind.[9] He is also seen as a psychopomp, detailed to stand at the crossroads of Paradise to guide the righteous dead to their appointed place. He is thus, like both Enoch and Merlin, a way-shower, guiding travellers on an inner journey; and, like Enoch, he rules over a portion of Paradise.

Many stories are told of Elijah's travels through the world, and of his many disguises, through which he becomes something of a joker – though always remaining a stern judge of human frailty.[10] Thus he is often to be found travelling the roads with some unsuspecting companion, behaving in an extraordinary manner or laughing unaccountably as one who knows the inner truth of the situation from an unknown source. In this he resembles Merlin closely, since there are several well-attested instances of 'Merlin's laughter', where he has perceived things unseen by others and finds the foolishness of men too funny to restrain his mirth.[11]

Indeed there are so many similarities between Elijah and Merlin that it is very easy to pass from one to the other, especially if one considers one of the most significant accounts of Merlin's end. It is found in the medieval Grail-Romance known as the *Didot Perceval*. Here Merlin declares that God 'did not wish him to show himself to people any longer, yet that he should not be able to die until the end of the world'.[12] To Perceval, he adds: 'I wish to make a lodging outside your palace and dwell there, and I shall prophesy wherever our lord commands me. And all those who see my lodging will name it the *Esplumoir* [or Moulting Cage] of Merlin.'[13]

Now with this word *Esplumoir* we come to the heart of the mystery which connects Merlin to the Inner Kings and at the same time provides the reason for his withdrawal.

Much speculation has gone into the meaning of the word.[14] What, after all, is this moulting cage? For a long while it was thought that the term originated from a falcon's cage, and that because Merlin happened to share his name with an actual bird of prey, that an elaborate pun was intended. In one sense this was right, since birds moult in order to change, to grow fresh plumage, and Merlin himself under another guise is described as wearing a cloak of feathers and living like a bird in a tree.

However, the real meaning of *Esplumoir* is even more complex, and takes us into some very strange areas. In Celtic tradition we find an episode from the *Voyage of Maelduin*[15] where the voyages arrive at an island where they see a huge bird renew itself in the waters of a lake. When one of the crew drinks this water he is said never again to be troubled with bad eyesight or toothache, so strong are the properties of the water. The same text adds a Biblical reference for the validity of this episode, from the psalm which says: 'You shall renew yourselves as eagles' and it is to a Biblical, or rather a Judaic, source that we must turn for a further definition of the *Esplumoir*.

In the *Zohar*,[16] one of the most important mystical texts of Judaism, we find a description of paradise which both recalls the earlier passages dealing with Enoch and Elijah, and takes us a step further. In this passage we read of a part of heaven in which is 'a certain hidden place, which no eye has seen but those to whom God shows it, and which is called "the Bird's Nest" ... within this the Messiah [in Jewish tradition there are many Messiahs, so that Christ is not necessarily meant here] lies ailing ... in the fifth hall of Paradise, in the castle of Souls, the Bird's Nest, visited only by Elijah, who comforts him'.[17]

This conjures up a scene which will be well known to students of the Grail. There, in many different texts, we find an old, ailing king, lying in the hall of the Grail castle (which could certainly be termed the Castle of the Soul) visited by Merlin. When we discover that, in a romance almost contemporary to the first known compilation of the texts which became the *Zohar*, this same king is called 'Messias' – a word which could only have come from the Hebrew – the parallel is even greater.[18]

What, then, of the 'Birds Nest'? The text further describes it as a place of prophetic vision:

> 'The Messiah enters that abode, lifts up his eyes, and beholds the Fathers [Patriarchs] visiting the ruins of God's sanctuary. He perceives mother Rachel with tears upon her face; the Holy One, blessed be He, tries to comfort her, but she refuses to be comforted. Then the Messiah lifts up his voice and weeps and the whole Garden of Eden quakes, and all the righteous saints who are there break out in crying and lamentation with him. When the crying and weeping resound for the second time, the whole firmament above the Garden begins to shake, and the cry echoes from five hundred myriads of supernal hosts, until it reaches the highest throne.'[19]

Merlin, also, when he enters his *Esplumoir*, is able to see things that others cannot: glimpses of British history just as the Messiah sees glimpses of Jewish history. There is, also, a marked similarity between the apocalyptic descriptions in the *Zohar* and the extraordinary visions of Merlin in both the *Vita Merlini* and the earlier *Prophecies* set out in Latin by Geoffrey of Monmouth, in the middle of the twelfth century.

Nor should we be surprised by these points of similarity between Christian and Judaic authorities; the barriers between the two cultures in the Middle Ages were far less severe than is often supposed. It is more than likely that any one of the widely read, much-travelled romance writers could have encountered the tradition embodied in the *Zohar* and elsewhere, and that it became a seed planted in the soil of their own vision.

In Celtic literature also, long recognised as a primary source for the Arthurian mythos, are descriptions of the Otherworld abode of the dead in which both Enoch and Elijah are described as living on a mysterious island until the Day of Judgement; and in an early poem of the bard Taliesin,[20] who also identified himself with Merlin, we find the line: 'I was instructor to Elijah and Enoch.'

Merlin likewise is said to retire to a glass house containing the Thirteen Treasures of Britain – including the Cauldron of Annwn, the Celtic Grail – and this also is on an island. (Indeed, an early nineteenth-century scholar interpreted this in his own particular way, describing 'a museum of rarities in King Arthur's time ... which Myrddin ap Morfran, the Caledonian, upon the destruction of that place, carried with him to the house of glass in the isle of Enill or Bardsey ... This house of glass, it seems, was the museum where they kept their curiosities to be seen by everybody, but not handled; and it is probable that Myrddin ... was the keeper of their museum in that time ...!')[21]

Seriously, however, Merlin's *Esplumoir* is here both a treasure house and a place of prophecy, as is the Bird's Nest, and within it, like Enoch and Elijah, Merlin notes down the history of mankind to a clerk named Helyas, whose name is itself a corruption of Elijah, and who writes down all that Merlin recounts from inside his retreat.[22]

Again, in the *Vita Merlini*, we have the description (so ably interpreted by Bob Stewart in his commentary on the book) of Merlin's observatory, to which he withdraws with his sister Ganeida, to study the heavens and the mysteries of creation.[23] Here, the moulting cage is a place of study and learning, a place where, in the magical inner realm built by Merlin himself in another dimension, the prophet and wise man can put together the fragments of his knowledge to make a whole. This is Merlin as Phoenix, and we may remember that in the German *Parzival* romance the Grail is described as a stone having the properties of renewal 'like that from which the phoenix renews itself when it is near to death, and from which it arises again restored'.

Before withdrawing, he was a king, but he rejects earthly sovreignty in order to discuss the meaning of meteorology or the purpose of the stars.

In the Jewish texts already quoted, we have seen that the Bird's Nest is a meeting place between the worlds; within the level of Paradise, or heaven, Enoch and Elijah enter the place where the Messiah sits, viewing the events of Creation. Is there anything within the stories of Merlin which further parallels this?

I believe there is. There are several references in Arthurian literature to an early name for Britain being *Clas Merddin*, Merlin's
Enclosure, and it is said elsewhere that he built a wall of brass around
this island to protect it from invasion or attack.[24] Here, I think, we
have the origin or seed-thought of the *Esplumoir*. Along with the
references to *Clas Merddin* are many more which relate the island of
Britain to the magical realm of Faery. In a text relating the adventures of Ogier le Dane, a hero once as famous as Arthur, we find him
carried off to Avalon by Morgan le Fay, the great enchantress of the
Arthurian legends. The description is interesting:

> 'The barge on which Ogier was, floated across the sea until it came near the
> Castle of Loadstone, which is called the Castle of Avalon, which is not far this
> side of the Terrestrial Paradise, whither were wrapt in a flame of fire Enoch and
> Elijah, and where was also Morgan le Fay ...'[25]

This is very much the kind of description one gets when the Otherworld is being talked of, and here we also find not only Morgan le
Fay but also both Enoch and Elijah.

Again, in the *Vita Merlini*, we find a description of Britain which
leaves us in no doubt that the tradition drawn upon here saw this
island in a particular light. Britain is:

> 'foremost and best, producing in its fruitfulness every single thing. For it bears
> crops which throughout the year give the noble gifts of fragrance to man, and
> it has woods and glades with honey dripping in them, and lofty mountains and
> broad green fields, fountains and rivers, fishes and cattle and wild beasts, fruit
> trees, gems, precious metals, and whatever creative nature is in the habit of
> furnishing.'[26]

This is Avalon as much as it is Britain; Merlin's isle, where adventure
begins at the stone that bears his name, and where his voice may be
heard upraised in prophetic utterance.

Together with Enoch, Elijah, Melchizadek and many more, Merlin
has become a withdrawn or Inner King indeed, one who has chosen
to enter an inner kingdom from which he will no longer play a direct
role in the affairs of the world, electing instead to mediate events

from a deeper level, where the barriers between humanity and the absolute are less defined.

This new house is the real *Esplumoir*, the moulting cage where we loose our ties with the world and move towards another state of being, guided by the withdrawn kings. There are parallels in many other areas of study, including Sufism or the Qabalah. This shifting jigsaw of people and places happens outside time, where different names are given to the same people, manifesting in time and at each junction taking on a new aspect with an ongoing purpose. Thus a late medieval manuscript source wonders that so wise a man as Merlin could have allowed himself to be entrapped by a girl, and speculates as to the real nature of the story. For,

> 'there are a variety of opinions and talk among the people, for some of them hold that ... Merlin was a spirit in human form, who was in that shape from the time of Vortigern until the beginning of King Arthur when he disappeared.
>
> After that, this spirit appeared again in the time of Maelgwn Gwynnedd at which time he was called Taliesin, who is said to be alive yet in a place called Caer Sidia. Then, he appeared a third time in the days of Morfran Frych son of Esyllt, whose son he was said to be, and in this period he was called Merlin the Mad. From that day to this, he is said to be resting in Caer Sidia, whence certain people believe firmly that he will rise up once again *before* Doomsday.'[27]

Note that word '*before*'. Merlin is evidently still seen as active from within the sphere of Caer Siddi – which is of course yet another name for the Celtic Otherworld, as well as a place where a famous prisoner, Gwair or Guri or Mabon, once resided.[28]

In the other, parallel version we have discussed, Enoch/Metatron begins as a replacement for Lucifer, righting the balance of power in heaven. He reappears as Melchizadek, initiating a line of priestly kings who lead to Christ, and beyond to the Grail itself. He reappears as Enoch, who becomes Sandalphon, the way-shower, returns yet again as Merlin, who takes the Grail to the Nesting Place, the Bird's Nest, the *Esplumoir,* from where it passes to other hands.

This is all a far cry from the view of a love-sick old fool who allows himself to be tricked into an imprisonment from which he cannot escape. I hope I have shown that Merlin's withdrawal is a willing one, made from choice, to allow him the freedom of spirit necessary to grow and change. This can best be brought about within the chamber of the Grail, which is called by many different names, but had only one identity, like the withdrawn kings.[29] They are the same, yet different, as is the Grail and all it stands for. Merlin is one of those figures who travel through the world for a while, only to withdraw again into the inner realm. This is how he was seen by the medieval writers who knew his story best; I believe it is how he should still be seen.

NOTES TO MERLIN'S ESPLUMOIR

1 *Vita Merlini*, Geoffrey of Monmouth, ed. and trans. J. J. Parry, University of Illinois Studies in Language and Literature, 1925. Edited with commentary *Mystic Life of Merlin*, R. J. Stewart, Arkana, 1986.
2 *Didot Perceval*, trans. D. Skeels. University of Washington Press, 1961.
3 Hebrews, chap. 7, v. 3.
4 Genesis, chap. 5, v. 24.
5 *The Legends of the Jews*, A. Ginsberg, pp. 138–9.
6 Ibid. pp. 139–40.
7 Ibid. pp. 137–40.
8 *Vita Merlini* op. cit..
9 Ginsberg op. cit. pp. 137–40.
10 Ibid. p. 139.
11 *History of the Kings of Britain*, Geoffrey of Monmouth; Penguin, 1966. Cf. Gaster, M. *Legend of Merlin* (in) *Folk-Lore* II, pp. 407–26, 1905. Also *Mystic Life of Merlin*, R. J. Stewart, chap. 5, 1986.
12 *Didot Perceval*, p. 94.
13 Ibid.
14. Cf. Adolf, H. *The Esplumoir Merlin* (in) *Speculum*, 1946, XXI, pp. 173–93. Also, Neitz, W. A. *The Esplumoir Merlin* (in) *Speculum* XVIII, 1943, pp. 67–79.
15 *Voyage of Maelduine* (in) *The Voyages of the St Brendan the Navigator* and *Tales of the Irish Saints* trans. Lady Gregory, Colin Smythe, 1973.
16 *The Zohar*, trans. H. Sperting and M. Simon, V, pp. 281ff. and III, pp. 21ff. 1931–34.
17 Ibid. III 22ff.
18 *The Vulgate Cycle of the Arthurian Romances*, ed. H. O. Sommer, The Carnegie Institution, vols. I and II, *L'Estoire del Saint Graal*, 1909–16.
19 *Zohar*, III, 22ff.
20 *Four Ancient Books of Wales*, ed. and trans. W. F. Skene, Edinburgh, 1868.
21 *Celtic Remains*, Silvan Evans, D. London, 1878.
22 *Prose Lancelot*, ed. and trans. L. A. Paton, George Routledge, 1929.
23 *Vita Merlini* op. cit.
24 *Parzival*, Wolfram von Eschenbach, trans. A. T. Hatto, Penguin, 1980.
25 *Le Roman d'Ogier le Danois*, fourteenth-century prose romance (unpublished).
26 *Vita Merlini* op. cit.
27 P. K. Ford, *The Death of Merlin in the Chronicle of Elis Gruffydd* (in) *Viator* no. 7, pp. 379–90, 1976.

28 *Mabon and the Mysteries of Britain*, C. Matthews, Arkana, 1987.
29 J. Matthews, *Temples of the Grail* (in) *At the Table of the Grail*, ed. J. Matthews, Arkana, 1987.

Grisandole (a story)

by John Matthews

Tell me this if you can: why should a woman want to be a man? Avenable did, though she was of noble blood and wanted for nothing. True, her father had been banished for some trifling offence and her circumstances were somewhat reduced, but she could still have lived out her life in a perfectly ordinary way: married, borne children, grown fat and eventually died, surrounded by a mourning husband, sons and daughters. Instead, she wanted to be a man 'to live in a man's world and experience all that men experience'. I can't see why she should have wanted that, since most men are such fools and seem to spend most of their lives hacking each other about with swords or trying to knock each other off their horses. As though it were *fun* to keep kissing the ground!

Still, Avenable was determined, and eventually her determination led her to run away and, having disguised herself as a youth, to take service in the Emperor's guard.

This is where the story becomes interesting, because at the time the Emperor was having a series of nightmares – or rather, the same nightmare over and over again, in which he saw a huge, rapacious sow being chased through the city by twelve boars. Of course, being an Emperor, he took this to be an omen of some kind, but could not find anyone brave enough to tell him whether it was for good or ill.

Of course, *I* knew what the dream meant, but I was not about to simply walk into the Emperor's court and tell him. However, there was an injustice to be set right; and there was Avenable – or rather Grisandole as she now called himself. So I quickly devised a plan to enable me to explain the dream, put right the injustice and show Grisandole the error of her ways.

The first anyone else knew of this was a few weeks later when the Emperor, his wife and their household – including of course Grisandole, were staying for a few days in one of his great country villas. There, just as the whole family were about to dine, there was a great commotion and a huge stag with vast branching antlers and one white foot burst into the hall and stood panting before the astonished people. It is said – and I will vouch for it because of course I *was* the stag: a mere matter of the transformative will – that the beast then spoke, telling the Emperor that it knew of his dreams and that only one person could tell him what they meant, and that was the Old Wise Man who lived in the depths of the forest near his palace. After which the beast vanished.

Of course, the Old Wise Man was me again, but no one would have believed me, let alone permitted me to get near the Emperor if I had simply wandered into the palace, or the villa, asking to see him. While I might indeed have used some other method, suitably spectacular, to gain admittance, this would not have solved the problem of Grisandole.

Well, in typically extravagant fashion the Emperor offered a huge reward to anyone who could find the Old Wise Man and bring him back for questioning. And of course everyone, including Grisandole, set off in search of the prophet; and of course they were unsuccessful – I am not someone to be found unless I want to be – which I did, in this instance, but not by just anyone.

I waited until most of the seekers had given up – though I kept on encouraging Grisandole, showing the occasional tip of an antler in the forest, or maybe the merest glimpse of an old ragged man – then I went to a clearing where I knew she was resting, and putting on the guise of the stag with one white foot again I told her what she must do to find and capture the Old Wise Man.

She was very obedient, was Grisandole, a sensible girl for all her strange fancies. She got five of her young companions-in-arms to come with her into the forest and set up a table with a white linen cloth over it and plenty of food. They lit a fire and sat down to wait.

Sure enough the Old Wise Man soon appeared, tucked into the meal and then went to sleep, snoring like a pig in front of the fire. It was an easy task for the six of them to bind me and then in the morning we all set off back to the Emperor's palace.

On the way three small events occurred, which I mention here only as an example of the way I like to work sometimes. Mystification is not enough, and being able to change one's shape or conjure things from the air isn't either.

The first incident was when we camped for the night in a field and Grisandole lay down with the other young men with me in the middle. I couldn't help laughing when I thought that not one of them knew she was a girl, and I suppose my laughter got the better of me, because in the end one of my companions came over and told me in no uncertain terms to keep quiet, waving a sword under my nose to make certain I understood.

The second incident was when we happened to pass a crowd of mendicants waiting for alms outside an abbey. They were a thin, unwashed, rather odorous bunch, and when I saw them – or rather when the Old Wise Man saw them – he began laughing so hugely that he almost fell off the horse on which he was tied. Grisandole and the rest looked at each other with the kind of looks that said: 'Ah, poor fellow, mad as a cuckoo.' But when the next incident occurred they seemed more concerned.

This was when we all stopped to hear Mass in a church along the way – some of the six wanted to give thanks for the reward they were going to get for finding me – and while we were in the church we saw a young squire leave his place three times, strike his astonished master a blow in the face and then stand there looking dazed, claiming that an unknown agency had made him do it.

No, it was not I, but I did start laughing again, so loudly that Grisandole took me outside, took out her sword and demanded to know what I was about. I didn't tell her, but I did call her a sly, deceitful villain, which not only made her angry, it also worried her in case I might somehow have penetrated her disguise. However, I refused to say another word, and in fact uttered not another sound until we reached the Emperor's palace, where I was led before him, still bound, and commanded to explicate the dream.

The exchange that followed went like this:

Emperor: Are you the Old Wise Man?
Me: URRGGHH!!!
Emperor: I see. And do you know the meaning of the dream I have had every night for a month?

Me: Ugghh!

Emperor: He is clearly mad. Take him away.

Me: I am most certainly not mad, sir. But I will only speak before all your nobles and your Empress and everyone of the court.

Emperor: Very well. We shall call our vassals before us on the morrow.

So I was taken away, given a bath – which truth to tell I was glad of, since playing flea-ridden old men is hard work even for me – then fed and given a clean and comfortable bed to sleep in. But an armed guard was placed on the door.

Next morning we all appeared before the Emperor in great splendour, including Grisandole with her armour polished so that you could see your face in it and her sword so sharp it would have cut the wind. They brought me in, and as soon as I saw the Empress I started laughing again, falling on the ground and rolling about, biting my beard like a madman. Which is what everyone thought I was, until I suddenly stopped, stood up and addressed the Emperor in my normal voice.

'Sir, I will explain everything to you. Those who brought me here will have told you of my laughter on other occasions. No doubt they thought me crazed. But each time there was a reason for my merriment. When we saw many men and women begging for bread and water, I laughed because all the time there was a treasure buried beneath their feet. Again we saw a squire who struck his master three times, and again I knew that beneath his feet lay a fortune – each blow that he struck was but a token of the evils of riches which cried out to him from the very earth. Now I laugh because of the meaning of your dream, which signifies this ...' I paused, I must admit, for effect, and knew that I had everyone's attention. Then I proceded to tell the Emperor that his Empress had twelve ladies-in-waiting who were in fact young men in disguise and that they had certainly been doing more than merely wait on her for the past six months. This was the meaning of the sow and the twelve boars which chased it through the city.

Uproar. Screams. Cries for mercy, death, clemency, execution. The Empress and her 'ladies' were held, examined and the truth found to be as I had described it. Then, while everyone was still gasping for breath, I told the Emperor about the other occasion when I had laughed – when I had looked at Grisandole sleeping between her sword-brothers and known that she was really a girl.

More uproar and outrage. But of course this time there was no real crime intended and Grisandole had served the Emperor well – apart from which, when he had a good look at her, the Emperor decided that Avenable, as we may call her again, was really rather beautiful, and that once the Empress had been executed for her crimes he would need a new consort; and as I said Avenable was very well connected.

I vanished, of course, leaving the usual cryptic message in letters of fire on the wall, to be interpreted later by a passing Latinist to the effect that Merlin was both the stag and the Old Wise Man.

As for the rest, Avenable's father was pardoned and his lands restored, while his daughter became the new Empress. As far as I know they are living happily enough. But I still cannot fathom why Avenable wanted to be a man, nor for that matter why she never seems to have forgiven me for setting her life in order. But I had other things to think about soon enough, what with young Arthur and all *that* entailed.

PART 6
ALBION

Introduction

by R. J. Stewart

Kathleen Raine's essay brings the entire range of discussion in both volumes of the *Book of Merlin* together in the remarkable figure of William Blake. Although there is no specific set of references to Merlin in this chapter, or to the Merlin texts, there is no doubt whatever that Blake embodied the primal prophetic and poetic traditions of which Merlin is the legendary master.

If we briefly consider the prophetic tradition manifesting itself through certain individuals, it seems clear that Blake is of the same lineage as Scotland's Robert Kirk (seventeenth century), or Thomas Rhymer (thirteenth century), but is a particularly English (although universal) seer and poet. We might even feel justified in suggesting that William Blake was the Merlin of his century ... no other visionary poet in Britain is comparable.

Just as the *Prophecies of Merlin* are couched in the confused remnants of bardic traditional symbolism, reworked by Geoffrey of Monmouth yet still representing a special alphabet of symbols partly lost and forgotten, so is Blake's prophetic work couched in a poetic alphabet of his own making, drawing upon enduring tradition. But in the case of Blake, as Kathleen Raine makes clear, the keys to this prophetic and symbolic alphabet remain clear and precise, accessible to the reader who makes the effort inwardly to awaken from spiritual sleep.

The Sleep of Albion

by Kathleen Raine

There is, in the treasury of every nation, a body of mythology, legend and folklore, interwoven with history and pre-history, associated with certain places and the names of kings and heroes, with events natural and supernatural, preserved by tradition both oral and recorded. These legends and records belong to the whole people, lending to each brief, unremarkable life a larger identity and participation, as if in some sense these stories were our own. They give us a place in history – and not merely in history but in a story whose imaginative meaning goes beyond history, lending a sense of glory and cosmic significance, and a beauty special to our own people and place on earth. Therefore we are considering a mass of material which, although it may have its basis in actual events, in real men and women who lived and loved and battled and quested, and who may very well be buried in the sites associated with them, eludes the kind of factual proof or disproof nowadays so popular with the excavators and researchers, all the error-proof techniques which modern fact finding demands. That the stories have been told and re-told is the only certain fact about them.

Such is what is known as the 'Matter of Britain', the corpus of British history and pre-history, as it has been handed down, and so designated in distinction from the 'Matter of Rome', established in the legends of the founding of the city of Romulus and Remus, fostered by the she-wolf, fit nurse of Rome's military genius; and the story of the conquest of Aeneas, refugee from Troy. France's 'matter' centres round Charlemagne and his knights; and the Teutonic nations likewise have their legendary history interwoven with myth and miracle – all those themes of Odin and Asgard, Siegfried and Parsifal which Wagner recreated in his opera.

The Matter of Britain, too, traces our origin back to Troy through the legendary Brut, who is said to have founded his kingdom in these isles; but also has roots in the prehistory and myths of the most ancient indigenous Celtic peoples, a marvellous mingling of Christian and pre-Christian themes.

Above all the Matter of Britain centres about a fifth-century Romanised British king or war leader, King Arthur, his chivalry, his court at Camelot, his Round Table, and the mysterious sanctity, neither wholly Christian nor wholly pagan, of the Holy Grail and its Quest. Doubtless there was a historical personage, a leader of cavalry as introduced and used by the Romans, at a time when the Saxon invaders fought on foot. Perhaps there was a Battle of Badon Hill in which the Saxons on foot were routed by a smaller number of mounted cavalry. There may even have been a Round Table, whether at Glastonbury or elsewhere, long turned to dust. But Arthur, the 'once and future king' of Britain, is far greater than any historical personage who may once have borne that name. Indeed the disentangling of the basis of historical fact from the whole tradition and literature of Arthur, his knights and his Round Table, would be an exercise in reductionism which could serve only to make him less 'real' as a presence, an archetype of kingship within the national imagination of the British people.

Rather than what remains when legend has been stripped away, King Arthur is the sum of all that has been recorded and imagined, written, told, sung and believed. He is a creation of, and a presence in, the national imagination, which has from century to century – even to the present day – continued to adorn Arthur and his court with all those attributes we would most wish to find in the person and circumstances of the perfect king. Arthur embodies the virtues of justice, fortitude, prudence and magnanimity as the British have conceived them; he commands the loyalty of knights of prowess, and establishes peace in his regions. Arthur's court, moving from place to place, confers its half-rustic splendour on these places where its joyous contests in arms and festivals shed a kind of beauty still somehow recognisably and specifically British, where good manners go hand in hand with good cheer.

The Arthurian cycle, for all the confusion and treachery of the king's overthrow by his nephew or son Mordred is a joyous one, not tragic like the story of Roland, nor bloodthirsty like the barbaric heroic Irish epic of Cuchulain and Queen Maeve. There is something of Shakespeare's Forest of Arden about Arthur's court. As for the 'Round Table', there are scholars who associate it with Near-Eastern legends of the King of the World whose Round Table is the zodiac and signifies spiritual world-rulership. Arthur's association with the constellation Arcturus, the Great Bear, casts his image as far as the stars, those enduring records of human dreams. There is something humane, pleasant, something of the English countryside in early summer (he held his court at the Feast of Whitsuntide) in Arthur's civilised yet rural kingdom. The British imagination has, in Arthur's kingdom of peace and justice, from Malory to Tennyson to the present day perfected an image of a ruler finely balanced between strength and mildness; an epitome, one might say, of the image of kingship latent in every Englishman.

The Matter of Britain remains very much alive in this country; one may cite John Cowper Powys's strange fantasy novel, *Porius*; T. E. White's *The Sword in the Stone* and its continuation in *The Once and Future King*; John Heath Stubbs's *Artorius* which some years ago won the Queen's Medal for poetry; and a recently published *Matter of Britain* by Harold Morland, not to mention the films *Camelot* and *Excalibur*. Towering among these is David Jones's *The Sleeping Lord*.

Myths and legends do not embody merely high ideals and things as moralists think they should be, however; the imagination of a race is much richer than that, and more mysterious. Arthur's marriage with Guinevere was flawed by the Queen's love for Launcelot du Lac, and by this knight's divided loyalty. Love, as is usually so in mythological stories, obeys laws of its own – Guinevere with her feminine un-law-abidingness is queen by right of that very independence of the moral law which she shares with Ireland's Queen Maeve, and Isolde, Queen of Cornwall, and with many a goddess. The Eternal Feminine is above, or beneath, or at all events outside all those laws, however admirable, that kings and law makers establish. Indeed the figures constellated about Arthur are scarcely less potent than the king himself – Gawain and Perceval and the other knights of the Grail quest; and Merlin the magician, type of the magical knowledge of the pre-Christian world, educator and adviser of the king. Merlin too is outside human law and order, reminding us that

Figure 10   The Old Man in the Forest

human rule is only relative and itself comprehended within a mystery which the magician may mediate but which neither he nor any human power can control. That kingship is itself decreed and bestowed by higher powers is implicit in that other familiar Arthurian story of the sword in the stone which could only be withdrawn by the divinely appointed heir to the kingdom.

Finally there is the legend of Arthur's death-sleep, somewhere in a secret cave where, with his knights around him, he awaits the time when he will return to restore just rule to his kingdom and to repel its enemies. It is above all this tradition of the sleeper who will wake at the time of need which lives on in the English imagination. Those of us who remember the Second World War remember how this myth was 'in the air' and cast its glamour on our great war leader Winston Churchill. Indeed this legend is never far below the surface in the national imagination; it is whispered that this or that royal prince may be Arthur returned to restore the kingdom to its golden age. Do people really believe this? Belief is probably the wrong word; not, certainly, as fact, but the archetype is a fact of the imagination and as such very real. Many are the places in England and Wales that claim to be the king's burial place. The sword Excalibur is said to have been thrown into Lake Ullswater (once within the boundaries of the British-Welsh kingdom) to summon the Three Queens in their boat. Also told in Northumberland is a story, recently re-told in his poem on the Matter of Britain by Harold Morland – which sites the cave where Arthur sleeps at Howsteads on Hadrian's Wall from Newcastle to Carlisle. It is said that a shepherd knitting a scarf as he tended his flock dropped his ball of wool, which ran away under the brambles and disappeared. The shepherd followed, and making his way through the tangled thicket came to a cleft in the rock through which he descended into a cave. There he saw the sleeping form of the king, and nearby a table on which was a sword and a horn. The shepherd took up the sword and struck the table. At this the king opened his eyes and half rose, only to say, 'You should have blown the horn', before falling back into his long sleep.

One recalls other legends of sleepers; there were the Seven Sleepers of Ephesus; the German Emperor Barbarossa; classical writers tell that the god Saturn himself sleeps in 'the Fortunate Isles' – Great

Britain – the god of the Golden Age which was once and will be again. Sometimes the sleeper is a figure of spiritual wisdom – Christian Rosencreuz, who sleeps in the sacred shrine of the Fama Fraternitatis, the Rosicrucians. Always there are the same stories, from the Cheviots to the Catskills, of some simple man who has come unawares upon the sleeper; and never is it certain where he lies. How different from the tomb of Napoleon, or of the Medicis, or of any of the great and illustrious figures of this world: The truly archetypal kings are not to be found in tombs like these, and about them always is an aura of the supernatural.

SACKED SITES

Both W. B. Yeats and his early friend the Irish mystic, AE, attached great importance to the sacred sites and holy places of Ireland; to 'marrying', as Yeats put it, the imagination of the people to lake and mountain and rock and river – to the land itself. The Holy Land of Christianity is elsewhere, in the Near East; for the Jews the land of Israel is their own land, the place of their ancestors; but for the Christian world Jerusalem and Sinai and Zion and Canaan are in effect – or were until this century for most untravelled human beings – imaginary places. Perhaps the persistence of the Arthurian legends we owe in part to the necessity for holy places in the very land we inhabit. The vision of the house of the Virgin Mary at Walsingham gave rise to the most famous place of pilgrimage of the late Middle Ages; a protest, by popular imagination, as it were, against the distancing of sacred sites from our own earth. When the Greeks sent out colonies the colonists would carry with them sacred fire, and would give the name of 'Mount Olympus' (where the gods live) to the nearest mountain worthy of the name. Blake writes of 'the council of God' meeting on 'Snowdon sublime', the highest peak in Wales and therefore fittest habitation for the spiritual guardians of Britain. This wedding of the imagination of a people to the earth itself serves not only to commemorate historic events and persons but also to give realities of the imagination (in Shakespeare's words) 'a local habitation and a name'. It does more – it makes a country, a landscape, a 'holy land', giving to mountains and rivers and springs and forests a dimension of the sacred – or shall we say, to put it at its lowest, a dimension of poetry?

Seen in this light some may regret that Milton abandoned his first intent of writing his great epic poem on the theme of King Arthur and chose instead *Paradise Lost*, imaginatively situated in regions remote from earth. Poetry cannot fulfil its task of giving to 'airy nothing a local habitation and a name' if the poet chooses to make theology his theme and all his characters save two disembodied spirits. Italy, France and other Catholic countries have succeeded to some extent in localising the Christian mysteries in their own towns and villages through painting and architecture, but in iconoclastic Protestant countries this has long ceased to be so; and since the Reformation Arthur and his Round Table, Merlin and the Holy Grail have remained our sole national heritage comparable with, for example, the Ramayana or the Mahabharata in India where real princes and charioteers merge with the world of the gods without losing their roots in history. The forests of Broceliande and of Brindaven are still real forests, to which the names of Merlin and Vivian, of the Lord Krishna and the Gopis, impart a mystery, a sacredness to the real forests of Brittany and of Orissa. When I saw in Delhi a wall said to have been built by the Pandavas, I had the awesome sense of myself entering the realm of myth.

I have long been struck by the fact that while the English and the Germanic nations have superficially so much in common there are deep differences in the archetypal figures that move under the surface, conditioning national character and national history. The figure of Faust, it is true, was the subject of Marlowe's play before Goethe gave to Faust and Mephistopheles that vitality Milton gave to Satan; but it is German writers and psychologists who are for ever composing variations on the theme of the pursuit of profane or forbidden knowledge. This restless activity of the godless mind of the human ego symbolised by Faust seems native and congenial to the German genius but has never in the same way (Marlowe notwithstanding) 'taken on' in England. It seems that our determining national archetype is that of the Sleeping King. It is not, it seems, the pursuit of forbidden knowledge but the tendency (like the dormouse in *Alice in Wonderland*) to fall asleep that besets the English. Perhaps Faust will one day be saved; and one day the sleeper of the ancient British kingdom will awaken. It is such themes as these which have been woven about the British king, whose legends have been preserved chiefly in Wales, custodian of the most ancient cultural deposits of the Celtic race which formerly occupied large areas of Great Britain.

BLAKE AND ALBION

William Blake, who called himself 'English Blake', emulated Milton in attempting a national epic on the theme not of history but of the spiritual destiny of the English nation in the group of so-called Prophetic Books of which one is entitled *Milton* and the last and most comprehensive, *Jerusalem*. Long incomprehensible because of their unfamiliar mythology whose action takes place not in history but in the inner worlds, Blake's mythological epics are none the less firmly rooted in national events – far more so than is *Paradise Lost*. The unfamiliar supernatural figures are those 'gods' or archetypal energies Blake discerned within the national collective life; and the central figure, whose inner drama is the theme of the whole action, is the 'Giant Albion', the collective person, so to speak, of the nation. Within his 'giant' body are comprehended all the cities and villages and mountains and regions of the British Isles, a national being of the many-in-one and one-in-many; and – perhaps this is not so much strange as inevitable – Blake, for all his admiration for Milton and his Christian faith, has reverted to the national myth of the Sleeping King. Albion is the sleeping giant (not a king, for Blake was a democrat) for whose re-awakening the 'four Zoas', and the other persons of the myth, labour. The Four Zoas are themselves extremely modern 'gods', corresponding as they do to the psychic functions of reason, feeling, sensation and intuition, made familiar in our century by C. G. Jung; but even these, as we shall see, have their roots in the 'matter of Britain' as Blake knew it.

Blake was versed in the Arthurian literature and traditions, and it is plain that the Sleeping Arthur is the model of the majestic sleeping form of the Giant Albion. Indeed among Blake's paintings exhibited in his exhibition in 1809 is one entitled *The Ancient Britons*, which in his catalogue he describes at length:

'In the last Battle of King Arthur only three Britons escaped; these were the Strongest Man, the Beautifullest Man, and the Ugliest Man. These three marched through the field unsubdued, as Gods, and the Sun of Britain set, but shall arise again with tenfold splendour when Arthur shall awake from sleep, and resume dominion over earth and ocean.'

There is no question but Blake's Albion is imagined in the similitude of Arthur; for in the same description (K. 577–8) Blake goes on to write:

'The British Antiquities are now in the Artist's hands; all his visionary contemplations, relating to his own country and its ancient glory, when it was, as it again shall be, the source of learning and inspiration. Arthur was a name for the constellation Arcturus, or Boötes, the keeper of the North Pole. And all the fables of Arthur and his round table; of the warlike naked Britons; of Merlin; of Arthur's conquest of the whole world; of his death, or sleep, and promise to return again; of the Druid monuments or temples; of the pavement of Watling-street; of London stone; of the caverns in Cornwall, Wales, Derbyshire and Scotland; of the Giants of Ireland and Britain; of the elemental beings called by us by the general name of fairies; and of these three who escaped, namely Beauty, Strength, and Ugliness.'

Thus at the time when he was already at work on his last Prophetic Book, *Jerusalem*, whose plot, so to say, is the sleep and awaking of Albion, the whole Arthurian 'matter' was uppermost in his mind. He goes on (K. 578) to write:

'The Giant Albion was Patriarch of the Atlantic; he is the Atlas of the Greeks, one of those the Greeks called Titans. The stories of Arthur are the acts of Albion, applied to a Prince of the fifth century, who conquered Europe, and held the Empire of the world in the dark age, which the Romans never again recovered.'

To the historian it might seem that Blake is here putting things the wrong way round, because the historical Arthur is 'real' and the Giant Albion 'imaginary'. But Blake was neither ignorant of history nor simple-minded; as he understood the matter the Giant Albion has the enduring reality of the collective identity and continuing life of the soul of the nation; whereas Arthur was only one individual in whom that soul once expressed itself and around whom the enduring reality of the national life crystallised, so to say. For Blake the Imagination is by no means 'imaginary'; a truth forecefully brought home to us in this century by the psychologists, and especially by C. G. Jung, who himself wrote of the 'transpersonal' or 'collective' mind which is shared by some family, tribe or nation, and is, finally, shared by the whole human race.

Henry Corbin the Ismaili scholar and metaphysician (and a member, with Jung, of the Eranos circle) employed the term 'imaginal' to avoid any ambiguity in the word 'imaginary' with its popular implication of something unreal. On the contrary, all these believed – and Yeats too stated his own belief (in *A Vision*) in the 'angels' who preside over nations – the archetypes of the Imaginal world are human reality itself, the stamp or imprint of human nature in us all. Therefore Blake, in seeing 'the Giant Albion' as the greater and more enduring reality, of whom Arthur was an embodiment and agent, about whose name the idea and ideal of English kingship gathered, is taking the deeper and truer view. The ever-popular reductionist methods of our excavators and researchers in sifting out the few grains of material (which can of course be found in any body of myth and legend) will have lost the reality of that which they set out to discover somewhere along the way. The Holy Grail is not some Bronze-Age cooking pot in a museum, nor a gold or silver chalice in church or shrine, but a reality that inspired the imagination of many at a certain period of history, and which continues to do so to this day. Wagner's Parsifal is no less living than the Perceval of the *Mabinogion*. Nor can the kingship of Arthur be dated: it is timeless in the imagination of the race. These legendary 'deposits' (to use a favourite word of their most recent bard, David Jones) are sacred stories of the British nation. Blake wrote (K. 579):

'The antiquities of every Nation under Heaven, is no less sacred than that of the Jews, they are the same thing, as Jacob Bryant and all antiquaries have proved. How other antiquities came to be neglected and disbelieved, while those of the Jews are collected and arranged, is an enquiry worthy both of the Antiquarian and the Divine. All had originally one language and one religion . . .'

Thus Blake in recounting 'the acts of Albion' considered himself to be recounting the sacred history – the inner history of the British nation from ancient times, with prophetic foresight of that future when Albion, like Arthur, is to wake from sleep. For all his great admiration for Milton – who himself becomes one of Blake's mythological persons – he himself departs from his model precisely in re-situating sacred history in England's green and pleasant land.

In his poem *Milton* Blake includes one of those passages which have so bewildered readers of a literal-minded kind in its combination of real places with mythological persons and events. So we see (M. 39, K. 531) Albion

'On his Couch
Of dread repose, seen by the visionary eye;
. . . his face is toward
The east, toward Jerusalem's Gates; groaning he sat above
His rocks. London & Bath & Legions & Edinburgh
Are the four pillars of his Throne; his left foot near London
Covers the shades of Tyburn; his instep from Windsor
To Primrose Hill stretching to Highgate & Holloway.
London is between his knees, its basements fourfold;
His right foot stretches to the sea on Dover cliffs, his heel
On Canterbury's ruins; his right hand covers lofty Wales,
His left Scotland; his bosom girt with gold involves
York, Edinburgh, Durham & Carlisle, & on the front
Bath, Oxford, Cambridge, Norwich; his right elbow
Leans on the Rocks of Erin's Land, Ireland, ancient nation.'

Thus England's Sleeping Lord covers all the isles and includes in his giant body all their inhabitants.

There are many places in the British Isles which claim the tomb of the sleeping Arthur; for Blake's Giant Albion the whole island is

his tomb (M. 15, 36, K. 497), the 'rock' of Britain in the Atlantic
Ocean washed by 'the Sea of time and space'.

> '... Albion upon the Rock of Ages,
> Deadly pale outstretch'd and snowy cold, storm cover'd,
> A Giant form of perfect beauty outstretch'd on the rock
> In solemn death . . .'

Sometimes the tomb is called 'the Sick Couch', for Albion's 'death'
is a spiritual malady, not a state of non-existence. Blake names the
poet Milton 'the awakener', for it is the poets who speak to the nation
with the voice of the Imagination (M. 20, 25, K. 502):

> '... Albion's sleeping Humanity began to turn upon his Couch,
> Feeling the electric flame of Milton's awful precipitate descent.'

Blake himself was an Awakener at a time he saw as the beginning of
a New Age – as witnessed by the American and French Revolutions;
England, as always, was slow to respond (M. 23, 3, K. 506);

> 'The trumpet of Judgment hath twice sounded: all Nations are awake,
> But thou art still heavy and dull. Awake, Albion, Awake!'

But Albion's time has not come; he 'turns upon his couch' then sinks
back 'in dismal dreams/Unawaken'd.'

The sleep of Arthur has not in itself any positive significance, and
is but the passing of time until the need of his nation summons him
to return. But the 'sleep' of the Giant Albion is conceived by Blake
not as the mere passage of time but as a state of apathy, of lowering
of consciousness, of forgetfulness of higher things. This element in
Blake's myth of the sleeping Albion does not come from the traditional 'deposits' of the Matter of Britain: it has another source, in
the writings of the Neo-Platonic philosophers, and especially of
Plotinus, in the translation made by his contemporary and one-time
friend Thomas Taylor the Platonist. Blake's theme of the sleep and
awakening of the soul of the nation embraces far more than the mere
return of the Once and Future King at the hour of need: Blake tells
the story of how the nation has come to lapse into spiritual ignorance

and forgetfulness, of the 'deadly dreams' of the deluded nation – all the cruelties of war and the injustices of peace that result from this alienation – and how the final awakening may come about not at the mere blowing of a horn but through the spiritual labours of the 'awakeners'.

This is not the occasion for describing the involved mythological happenings of the Giant Albion's long 'dream' in the course of the 'deadly sleep' of his wanderings from eternal life. Blake's first version of the theme, *Vala or the Four Zoas*, announces the theme (FZ. 1, 21–25, K. 264) as Albion's

> '... fall into Division & his Resurrection to Unity:
> His fall into the Generation of decay & death, & his
> Regeneration by the Resurrection from the dead.'

His last Prophetic Book, *Jerusalem*, he introduces (J. 4, 1–2, K. 622) in a similar way:

> 'Of the Sleep of Ulro! and of the passage through;
> Eternal Death! and of the awaking to Eternal Life.'

For Blake the 'fall' is not, as for Milton, a fall into sin through disobedience, but a fall into 'sleep' through a closing of consciousness and loss of the 'divine vision' (FZ. 1, 290, K. 272):

> 'Refusing to behold the Divine Image which all behold
> And live thereby, he is sunk down into a deadly sleep.'

The 'divine image' is the archetype of human nature imprinted in every soul, as described in the first chapter of *Genesis*. Blake nowhere writes of the 'Fall' in terms of Christian theology (as Milton does) through man's disobedience and sin; rather he adopts the Platonic view of the human condition as one of forgetfulness of eternal things. All know Plato's myth (in the Tenth Book of the *Republic*) of the souls who, as they approach generation, reach a river – the river of forgetfulness, where all must drink. Some drink deeply and their forgetfulness of eternity is complete. Others, who wisely refrain from drinking so deeply, retain some memory of eternal things. These are the philosophers, the lovers and the musical souls who retain the vision of eternal things. For Blake held that the soul knows everything, and needs only to remember what it already and for ever knows – a view, besides, more in keeping with modern psychology which also sees unconsciousness rather than 'original sin'.

Blake's own prophetic task – as of all poets of the imagination – he saw as that of the Awakener; he summons Albion (J. 4, 6, K. 622):

'Awake! awake O sleeper of the land of shadows, wake! expand!'

and he announced his own prophetic task (J. 5, 17, K. 623):

'... I rest not from my great task!
To open the Eternal Worlds, to open the immortal Eyes
Of Man inwards into the Worlds of Thought, into Eternity
Ever expanding in the Bosom of God, the Human Imagination.'

Albion's sleep is the 'deadly sleep' of a narrowed and closed vision; the awakening of the Sleeping Lord is a stirring into life of the soul of the nation; it concerns us all.

THE IDEOLOGIES OF ALBION

Albion's 'deadly sleep' is a dire reality of national life, troubled with 'dreams'. It is a state of illusion, a loss of the 'divine vision' in which the nation falls under the power of 'the mind of the natural frame', of the empirical ego, called by Blake the 'selfhood' or Satan. Blake is quite specific in his diagnosis of England's national disease: it is precisely that secular materialism (which Blake associated with the honoured names of Bacon, Newton and Locke) upon which modern Western civilisation is founded; and has foundered, some would now say, Blake's prophetic vision having proved truer than his contemporaries could have foreseen. When natural reason usurps the place of imaginative vision and announces 'Now I am Good from eternity to eternity', and the 'divine vision' innate in every soul fades from consciousness, the rest follows. This *hubris* of natural reason in its pursuit of natural knowledge outside the context of spiritual wisdom has brought consequences which may well appal us. This Blake had understood at a time when triumphalist mechanistic science was still in its infancy.

Again, readers of Blake are shocked when from the charmed regions of mythology we are suddenly jolted into awareness that Blake is talking about realities – ideologies – well known to us and propounded daily on the media with all the assurance of received majority opinion. The 'mind of the natural frame', Urizen – Satan as he is named in the later Prophetic Books – is called 'Newton's Pantocrator, weaving the woof of Locke'. He is opaque to spiritual knowledge, recognising only natural fact, and is the very spirit of modern reductionism. Have we not all heard the voice which for Blake (J. 33, 5. K. 659) is the very voice of Satan, denying the innate divine humanity:

> I am your Rational Power, O Albion, & that Human Form
> You call Divine is but a Worm seventy inches long
> The creeps forth in a night & is dried in the morning sun,
> In fortuitous concourse of memorys accumulated & lost.
> It plows the Earth in its own conceit, it overwhelms the Hills
> Beneath its winding labyrinths, till a stone of the brook
> Stops it in midst of its pride...'

Blake thought otherwise: it is vision, not scepticism, which is wise. 'This', he wrote (*Everlasting Gospel* h. K. 756), 'was spoke by My Spectre to Voltaire, Bacon, & ...

> 'Did Jesus teach doubt? Or did he
> Give any lessons of Philosophy,
> Charge Visionaries with deceiving,
> Or call Men wise for not Believing?'

The sleep of Albion is in a word the materialist mentality of the modern West, it is this mentality which has taught the Children of Albion 'To converse concerning Weight & Distance in the Wilds of Newton & Locke' (K. 661) in a world of quantity outside 'existence' for, Blake asks, 'where is the existence outside mind and thought?' The quantification of nature, as something existing outside mind and thought, is literally soul destroying, a 'wrenching apart' of outer and inner worlds in which nature becomes a lifeless mechanism and the soul Descartes' *'folle du logis'* – the madman in the house. We have in our own time witnessed the logical outcome of this mechanisation of nature in the mechanisation of humanity itself; while at the same time we attribute to pieces of mechanism the human attributes of mind and thought. Could any idolatry be more abject than the present-day idolatry of the machine? All this, in its deadly ramifications, Blake has mythologised in his account of the 'sickness of Albion'.

In thus making humanity passive before a mechanised nature (so Yeats puts it) the original unity of being, of man and his universe, inner and outer, has been destroyed; and it is this restoration which will awaken Albion – and his 'sickness' has by now infected the whole of the modern world – from his deadly sleep, his oblivion which has turned his paradise into a desert (J. 19, 10, K. 641):

> 'The corn is turn'd to thistles & the apples into poison,
> The birds of song to murderous crows, his joys to bitter groans,
> The voices of children in his tents to cries of helpless infants,
> And self-exiled from the face of light & shine of morning,
> In the dark world, a narrow house! He wanders up and down
> Seeking for rest and finding none!'

Before this externalisation of nature by the post-Cartesian objectivity whose English equivalents were Bacon, Newton and Locke, the universe was one with humanity. In his address 'To the Jews' with which Blake introduces the Second Book of *Jerusalem* he again alludes to the one universal tradition, claiming that Britain was the original seat of that 'everlasting Gospel'(K. 649):

'Jerusalem the Emanation of the Giant Albion! Can it be? Is it a Truth that the Learned have explored? Was Britain the Primitive Seat of the Patriarchal Religion? If it was true ... Ye are united, O ye Inhabitants of Earth, in One Religion, The Religion of Jesus, the most Ancient, Eternal & the Everlasting Gospel ... All things Begin & End in Albion's Ancient Druid Rocky Shore.'

Blake then goes on to declare that the Hebrew patriarchs learned from 'the Druids', who were priests of this universal religion, and he equates the Adam Kadmon of the Jewish mystical tradition with the Giant Albion; the two symbols having the same significance of the primordial universal humanity (K. 649):

'You have a tradition, that Man anciently contained in his mighty limbs all things in Heaven & Earth; this you received from the Druids. "But now the Starry Heavens are fled from the mighty limbs of Albion".'

This externalisation of the natural universe is illustrated in Plate 25 of *Jerusalem* where Albion is depicted with sun, moon and stars in his 'mighty limbs' from which they are being separated by females representing the agents of natural generation. Now the post-Cartesian phase of Western thought has run its course, and science itself is confronted, in many fields, with the realisation (so plain to Blake) that the object of knowledge cannot be separated from the mind that knows. Can it be that Albion is stirring in his 'sleep' of materialist oblivion? Blake prayed (J. 15, 10, K. 633) for the divine Spirit for inspiration,

'That I may awake Albion from his long & cold repose;
For Bacon & Newton, sheath'd in dismal steel, their terrors hang
Like iron scourges over Albion . . .'

and he indicts the 'schools and universities of Europe' (J. 15, 14, K. 636):

'I turn my eyes to the Schools & Universities of Europe
And there behold the Loom of Locke, whose Woof rages dire,
Wash'd by the Water-wheels of Newton; black the cloth
In heavy wreathes folds over every Nation: cruel Works
Of many Wheels I view, wheel without wheel, with cogs tyrannic
Moving by compulsion each other, not as those in Eden, which,
Wheel within Wheel, in freedom revolve in harmony & peace.'

Let us not forget that Blake's phrase, the 'dark Satanic mills' refers
not to the landscape of the Industrial Revolution but to the mechanistic ideology which created that landscape. Here he contrasts the
opaque 'black cloth' turned out by the Universities with the 'wheel
within wheel' of Ezekiel's vision of the 'living creatures' and their
wheels within wheel. He would see the same black cloth coming from
the looms of the Universities to this day and not only those of
Europe. But need I say more? These things are well known to us all.

Albion's state of 'eternal death' therefore is seen not in terms of
some comfortably remote myth but clearly and precisely identified
as the materialist ideology to which the West has succumbed.

THE SLEEPERS

There is of course only one sleeping King Arthur; but Blake writes
of many 'sleepers' who are the individual lives within the national
being; and here again he is close to Plato and Plotinus, who are
concerned with individual souls, who as they descend into generation
lose their consciousness of eternal things and become 'sleepers'.
Plotinus writes of those who transmigrate from one incarnation to
another, passing 'as it were from bed to bed, from sleep to sleep';
and Blake too writes of these 'sleepers' who enter the world of
generation, whom he calls 'the spectres of the dead'. He describes in
Milton (M. 26, 26, K. 512), in terms rather Platonic than Christian,
how the souls 'descend' into this world,

> '... being piteous Passions & Desires
> with neither lineament nor form, but like to wat'ry clouds
> The Passions & Desires descend upon the hungry winds,
> For such alone Sleepers remain, meer passion & appetite.'

The Sons of Los, Blake's time-spirit, take charge of these pathetic
spectres, clothe them, and give them gardens and fields – not of the
kind that can be bought from the estate agent, but works of art,
paintings, poetry and music they can 'inhabit'; for poetry, as I. A.
Richards somewhere says, is the house of the soul. Blake describes
how Milton himself, for Blake the supreme poet, whom he calls 'the

awakener', takes on a human body and thereby enters the state of 'sleep'; but in his sleep he is fed by the angels with 'food of Eden', visions of eternal things.

> 'As when a man dreams he reflects not that his body sleeps,
> Else he would wake, so seem'd he entering his Shadow: but
> With him the Spirits of the Seven Angels of the Presence
> Entering, they gave him still perceptions of his Sleeping Body
> Which now arose and walk'd with them in Eden ...'

Milton's 'real and immortal Self' appeared to 'those who dwell in immortality', Blake writes (M. 151, 15, 12–16, K. 496),

> '... as One sleeping on a couch
> Of gold, and those in immortality [that is the Seven Angels] gave forth
>   their Emanations
> Like Females of sweet beauty to guard round him & to feed
> His lips with food of Eden in his cold and dim repose:
> But to himself he seem'd a wanderer lost in dreary night.'

The poet, inspired as he may be by the Muses, can see in his imagination lost Eden, but is none the less an exile in this world, in his natural humanity. But it is Milton and the other poets and visionaries who still in dreams behold eternity who labour to clothe and build houses for the 'spectres of the dead' whose sleep is absolute; until 'a vast family, wondrous in beauty and love' is created on earth. So through the infinite labours of love the dead are awakened to life through recollection of eternal things, depicted in works of art. For 'what', Blake asks (J. 77, K. 717),

> 'What is Mortality but the things relating to the Body which Dies? What is Immortality but the things relating to the Spirit which Lives Eternally? What is the Joy of Heaven but Improvement in the things of the Spirit? What are the Pains of Hell but Ignorance, Bodily Lust, Idleness & devastation of the things of the Spirit?'

Blake believed that 'Albion shall rise again' because our human nature and its innate potentiality is what it is, no matter what we believe or disbelieve. Things are as they are and we need only – in

Platonic terms – remember that we already and for ever know. It is not because of what materialist science contains, but because of what it excludes that Blake attacks the materialist view; which takes a part of knowledge for the whole, oblivious, in its 'deadly sleep', of those 'worlds of thought' which it was Blake's prophetic task to open. Blake calls upon the nation to listen to its poets, painters and musicians – and also to its religious visionaries, like Whitfield and Wesley – who bring news from lost Paradise. It is these who are 'awake' to the regions of the human imagination which for the materialist mentality are a lost and forgotten country. By deifying natural reason, 'the true man', who is much greater and more comprehensive than the empirical ego whose only source of knowledge is through the senses ('a fortuitous concourse of memorys accumulated and lost') is excluded from consciousness. The only knowledge of the empirical ego is what the senses bring from an externalised and lifeless material universe. Our humanity, Blake understood, is far greater than we know.

The awakening of the sleeper, therefore, calls for no change in outer circumstances, in the 'conditions' of our work or the size of our income, better roads, housing and the like, still less any of those products of the machine offered in such profusion by their manufacturers. No, what is called for is a change in our consciousness itself, that will make us aware of what is daily before our eyes – the rising and setting sun, the clouds, the moon and stars, the tree outside the window.

For Blake (Notebook pp. 80–81, K. 609) the arts are something far other than 'entertainment' or 'self expression': they bring news from lost Paradise, which the poets continue to see afar off while the 'sleepers' have forgotten: '... Poetry, Painting & Music, the three Powers in Man of conversing with Paradise, which the flood did not Sweep away.' Paradise is not a place but a state of being to which the myriad sleepers of Albion must someday awake.

Blake was himself a poor and obscure man but he possessed the secret of being happy in this world; no special privileges are needed, for sun and moon, wild flower and grain of sand, are here for us all; but many find it easier to demand better 'conditions' in the outer world than to make the effort necessary to see the 'innumerable company of the heavenly host'. The awakening of the sleepers does call for effort. When Blake asks for 'the liberty both of body and mind to exercise the Divine Arts of Imagination' he is really laying the onus on ourselves to exercise those divine arts; no easy task – he is asking a great deal of us, and he summons each of us, 'as much as in him lies' to 'engage himself openly & publicly before all the World in some Mental pursuit for the Building up of Jerusalem' (J. 77, K. 717). We ourselves are the sleeping Albion, and it is for us to bring back the nation to that lost kingdom. For Blake that kingdom is the New Jerusalem itself, the kingdom of the human Imagination. Therefore it follows: 'A Poet, a Painter, a Musician, an Architect; the Man Or Woman who is not one of these is not a Christian' (Laocoön, K. 776). Blake's simplicities, we may feel, are more disconcerting and more demanding than his obscurities.

PART 7
MERLIN AND
THE MOTHER GODDESS

Introduction
by R.J. Stewart

We now encounter the complex traditions relating to Merlin that are found within modern magical or Western esoteric orders. Many writers or students of tradition ignore the fusion of lore found in magical groups and literature, mainly because so much of the material contained therein is blatant nonsense; but Dolores Ashcroft-Nowicki has summarised the entire range of teachings relating to Merlin that a student in a modern magical order might be expected to absorb before moving on to more specific or advanced aspects of the Mysteries.

This body of lore is a kind of sub-tradition, a special branch of the enduring collective traditions that range through time. It contains many of the familiar aspects of Merlin that we know through Celtic and medieval literature, but also contains a number of quite independent teachings, stories and poetic themes, handed down within modern esoteric groups.

It would be quite wrong to suggest that these independent teachings are fabrications, merely because no datable literary source may be found for them in antiquity or in early manuscripts preserved in museums and libraries. There are at least three theoretical sources for Merlin traditions in magical orders, and these may be summarised as follows:

1) Variations on early texts and traditions which may be traced to original sources. These can, of course, include modern literature.
2) Poetic or meditative regeneration of specific themes, legends, symbols and insights. Such regenerations, which are simply a matter of collective story telling at its most primal, always occur within any group or society, and revolve around its focus of special interest ... in this case Merlin.

3) Teaching or communication from inner-world sources (partly discussed in the Merlin context by John Matthews in Part 5).

This last category is the one most open to trivia and abuse, but must be considered as a source of folklore, in the sense of material circulated within a special group, even if we do not necessarily accept theories regarding its significance, effect, or ultimate source.

Dolores Ashcroft-Nowicki is well qualified to make the vital distinctions between valid magical teaching and superficial fantasy communication. In her chapter, she concentrates specifically upon the spiralling relationship between Merlin and the Mother Goddess, casting her net across the wide stream of Merlin stories that runs from the Celtic past into the present day of novels, films and television; but she never loses sight of the central potent teaching, that Merlin gained his wisdom through relationship to the Goddess, to the women in his life and the feminine principle of consciousness and energy. Thus this last chapter of original material brings our subject full circle, to Merlin and Woman.

Merlin and the Mother Goddess
by Dolores Ashcroft-Nowicki

'Whom does the Grail serve?' So goes the momentous question in the Grail saga; but we might ask another question, one more low key perhaps, more subtle, less obviously part of the whole Arthurian/ Merlin story, yet just as important to a full understanding of its message: 'Whom does Merlin serve?'

To find the answer we must reach back much further than the small space of time taken up by the Arthurian cycle. That could only have occupied what we must assume to be the last twenty years or so of his life, I assume, for while tradition holds that he withdrew from mortal eyes, it does not say that he actually died. Rather it tells us that he entered another dimension of existence, something that has been said of many men and women before and since. It was said of Enoch and Elijah, of the Beloved Disciple, of Prester John, of Balkis, the Queen of Sheba, and many of the hero kings who chose to withdraw in a like manner. No, the answer to our question lies in the early life of Merlin, starting with his birth, an event that has been greatly misconstrued and overlaid by successive writers. The earliest of these would have been clerics dedicated by reason of their calling to the 'demonising' of the pagan priesthood that had reigned and taught before them.

There is a great deal of precedence to show that the ritual conception of a child destined for a special task was an accepted part of many ancient mystery religions. Both parents were chosen for their inherent psychic powers as well as for their physical perfection, for anything less than that was unthinkable in one conceived for a life of special service. Priests of both sexes fully understood that they might be called upon for such a ritual at any time during their reproductive lives; to them it would have been as normal and as honourable as a life spent in an enclosed order is to a devout Roman catholic today. As with all religious practices at one time or another the 'Great Ritual of Hathor', or as it was more simply called 'The

Great Rite', was abused, twisted and gradually degenerated, though there were always those who kept alive the pure form of the Rite and the ideals that underlined it.

In its early days the use and power of the Great Rite was understood the length and breadth of the known world at that time and its requirements were always the same. Both those concerned had to be willing to offer themselves to its purpose, both had to be psychically active and highly trained, healthy and unblemished. One and sometimes both were masked to accentuate the atmosphere of otherworldliness, and lastly the priestess had to be virgin, a clean vessel that, to use the ancient definition of the word, belonged to no man but who was her own person.

The child born of such a union was held to be something more than human, semi-divine, a child of the gods themselves, and who is to say that this was not so? All the great religions have held to the same pattern, the unknown and 'divine' father, the willing sacred virgin dedicated to her accepted task, the child born into the world and yet existing outside it in some mysterious way by reason of its strange conception. Set apart for a lifetime of service and in most cases denied many of the human comforts of life and love, and often destined to die a sacrificial and painfully degrading death.

In rare cases such children became the great teachers and saviours of their age, others were born for less momentous tasks, but tasks that nevertheless were of great importance. Merlin, I submit, was one such. We do not know if the Merlin of British legend was the original one of that name; it has been suggested that it was a title rather than a personal name. That must be left for others to expand upon – my concern here is to seek an answer to the question posed at the beginning of this chapter. To that end let us look at the circumstances of Merlin's birth and parentage and see what they can tell us.

Legend states that Merlin's mother was a Welsh princess, or at least of noble birth, and that she was visited by a demon, one of the Lords of Hell, who wooed her in the guise of a handsome lad. The aim, so the early Christian clerics held, was to bring about the birth of the anti-Christ. This plan was thwarted at the last moment when the young mother, or in a different version her aged confessor,

Figure 11   The Mother Goddess, from the Prophecies of Merlin

recognising the child's demonic inheritance, baptised it as soon as it was born. Now the young Merlin existed in two worlds, that of his mother by reason of his new baptism, and that of his father by inclination, temperament and blood. One might suppose that such a confrontation would have cancelled out any powers he may have been born with, and that he would have spent his days either as a minor bastard princeling, or bundled off to a monastery as soon as it was convenient, or he was old enough.

The Cymri of ancient times, however, did not accept Christianity as quickly as the church would have us believe. It is far more likely that the young and virginal princess was dedicated from birth to the service of the Goddess. She would have been called, as were the priestesses of the Temple of Naradek in ancient Atlantis, to walk, accompanied only by the High Priest of the Rite, the dark, lonely way between the House of the Virgins and the sacred grove where the Rite and an unknown priest of the Old Religion awaited her. She would have returned in the early light of dawn, a maid no more but something far greater. The future mother of one destined to be not just a teacher and friend of kings, but one whose very name would become part of Britain's heritage. All through the long dreaming months ahead she would have pondered on the future of the babe she carried, and she would not have been human had she not wondered who had fathered him, just as another young woman centuries before in Palestine had 'held these things and pondered them in her heart'.

When her child was born he would have been received with great joy as the Returning Son/Sun, the living proof that their ways would survive for another generation at least. Because the old ways were already under siege it would have been deemed necessary to have the child baptised into the new religion that was gaining a swift foothold everywhere. Thus placed under the auspices of the church and further protected by his mother's noble bloodline and position as a priestess, Merlin's unknown parentage would have caused but little stir. There were still many who adhered to the Old Ways and their practices; to them he would have been a Divine Child to be regarded with awe and not a little pride.

The first five to seven years of his life would have been spent in his mother's care and his progress carefully monitored. For him the carefree days of childhood would have been but few; a lifetime's work lay ahead of him, and there was much to learn. His first tutors would have been his mother and the Priest of the Rite, and perhaps his unknown father, all eager to teach him the Magical Art that was part of his inheritance.

His Christian baptism put him in a unique position, as his protectors well knew. He was a 'firstfooter' a 'Walker between the Worlds', the one that was passing and the one still to make his presence felt. A herald of the new age, and a symbol of the old one, belonging partly to both and fully to neither. It was his destiny to train the last Sacred King born of the Great Rite as he himself had been born. To establish a Pattern on earth that would reflect the same Pattern above, the Table Round, the Sacred Cup flattened out but still acting as a container wherein many were gathered together. His was also the task to build the Gateway to the Innerworld place where the Sacred King, the Wounded One, might rest until he was healed and his time came again. At this point it is also interesting to note that Merlin in the course of his life-time's work dealt with many changes of the Grail, the Stone, into which is thrust the sacred Lance or the Sword of Kingship, the Child/Arthur, the Platter or Table Round and the Grail itself which he foresaw in vision.

From the legends passed down to us it would seem that Merlin's talents flowered early, as well they might in the 'Child of a Royal Virgin'. Like another boy who was found teaching the teachers at the age of twelve, he was soon put to the test. His reputation as the son of an unknown father brought him to the notice of the usurper King Vortigern, who ordered the presence of both Merlin and his priestess mother. She was to answer the charge of being in league with the devil, and her son was to be the sacrifice whose blood would build the king's new fortress. Merlin, however, had been well trained and, using his psychic skills, proved himself considerably more adept at the art of prophecy than those who were advising the king. It seems strange that a mere child, as the legend tells us, should be found in such a position, but then severe tests are required of all his kind from an early age.

From this time his mother fades from the story, as one would

expect, for now Merlin begins his Rite of Passage, the first require-
ment of which is the breaking away from all that is known and loved.
We see this in all such lives of destiny and especially in the Arthurian
texts. Perceval left his mother despite her pleas. Lancelot was stolen
by the Lady of the Lake. Galahad's destiny took him from his mother
Elaine. The Mother is the first of all teachers, she is also the last
teacher of all. She is the Giver of Gifts, the twin gifts of life and
death.

Merlin must now make his own mistakes and learn wisdom in the
making of them, but the Female image will still guide his footsteps
as he moves towards his destiny. In his life women played an important part, women of the real world and those of the land of Faerie. It
was also required of him, as it was with all priests of the ancient
world, to deal with and learn from his own secret inner female self,
his magical 'anima'. To learn from ... and perhaps to fear as men
sometimes do when faced with their inner feminine power, yet it
must be faced and accepted, for without the totality of balance then
achieved, the highest paths of Magic cannot be trodden with any
degree of safety.

It is time now to ask the question again: 'Whom does Merlin
serve?' Now we have the answer. He serves the Great Mother, the
Lady of Sorrows, the Giver of Life and Death, and in serving her he
also serves humankind as a whole. Like all who serve her, he is the
servant, the teacher, the guide, but never the ruler, never the King,
standing in the shadows observing, suggesting, always apart and
always alone. Unlike the Priest of the Sun who may be both priest
and king, the Priest of the Moon works from behind the scenes,
quietly and without pomp.

Having sought and found the answer to our question we find
ourselves faced with another. 'How is the Great Mother served?'
Because of the circumstances of his birth we may assume that Merlin
was born for a particular undertaking, and our next task is to search
out what that might be. When we look at the highlights of the
Arthurian cycle we can plot a series of events that indicate a certain
source of Inner Level Power. If we look at his own birth and its
mysteries and then move forward in time to the conception of Arthur,
we can see there are similarities that leave us in no doubt that here

was a repetition of those same circumstances, with one exception. Ygraine was not a virgin priestess, but a married woman who had already, so we are told, born a child, a daughter called Morgan or Morgause.

The value of Ygraine's participation is her blood line, linking her to the ancient Sea-Kings of the Drowned Lands, the oldest royal line of the West. To join such an ancient lineage with that of Uther Pendragon was to plan the creation of a dynasty of enormous power, both temporal and spiritual. The child of such a pairing would be the Once and Future King whose coming had been planned by the Goddess for many centuries. Such was to be Merlin's task. He, trained as a Priest of the Moon, was to arrange the match, oversee the Great Rite and then return to claim the child at birth and spirit him away as he himself had been taken to begin the long and arduous training for his priesthood under the 'Lake'.

Perhaps it was at this point that the deviation began to show. Did the purely human side of Merlin falter in its perception or values? Or did Uther, without the benefit of Merlin's kind of training, plan it so? We will never know for sure; but I think we must make the assumption that the death of Gorlois was not part of Merlin's scheme and that this one event was the basic flaw that was to mar the whole plan. Otherwise the child could easily have been passed off as being that of Gorlois until the birth, when it would probably have been claimed a 'stillbirth' and the babe given to Merlin as planned. But Gorlois was slain and too many people had seen him killed at the same time that he was 'seen' in the Queen's chamber. There was no way around it, the child was known to be Uther's, but born out of wedlock ... a 'bastard' as indeed was Merlin himself.

The child was born and Merlin took him and placed him with those who would care for him until his young manhood. Merlin himself now seems to disappear for a period of time. Where did he go during those long years? Did he move about the land working enchantments and going about the business of The Lady, and during the process becoming known as the Archmage of Britain? Did he return to those who had trained him, to wait until needed? Did he travel between the worlds where live those Fair Folk who are also a part of the history of the Blessed Isles, learning from them and joining in their music and revels? Or did he perhaps start upon the next task, the conception of Arthur's bride to be? If so, who was she? It is certain that Merlin warned Arthur against marrying Guenevere, so she could not have been his, Merlin's, choice of bride, but who was his choice, or perhaps we should say who was the choice of the Goddess, for She it is who is now seen as the guiding star of the Blessed Isles?

Need we look further than Elaine, the Grail Maiden, daughter of the Guardian of the Grail, whose lineage was impeccable and who would have brought with her as a dowry the Castle of the Grail itself and the title of the 'Grail King' for her husband? The son born of such a union would have been a true Priest-King combining the old ways and the new, a scion of the ancient Atlantean line and that of the Sacred Kings. A Priest of the Sun/Son who might well have brought the Grail, symbol of the Moon and the Great Mother, to full manifestation on earth. One, moreover, who had been born according to the Great Rite, watched over and guided by Merlin, the Priest of the Moon, and the Server of the Great Mother.

All this might have been but for the echo of a long-forgotten incident . . . the killing of Gorlois all those years before. Actions cause reactions not only in the world of magic but through all the existing worlds, level after level after level, and one mistake may cause ripples weft of time that can affect lives for generations. Morgana, the daughter of Gorlois and Ygraine, had neither forgotten nor forgiven the killing of her father and after all the intervening years still held Merlin to blame. Her instrument of revenge was to be the child whose conception and birth he had overseen: Arthur.

As with all archetypes the Great Mother exists as a duality. Her power may be called upon and used for both good and evil according to the will of the one using that power. Morgana certainly had enough of her mother's blood in her to tap such power and all the legends speak of her ability in the magical arts. Her method of revenge was to seduce her half-brother, stealing not only his boyhood innocence but also the seed that would have belonged by right to his Queen. The conception that Merlin in his role of Priest of the Great Mother should have consecrated became instead a deed committed in darkness, and without the blessing or the protection he could have provided. Instead of the Grail Prince, the Sun Child, Arthur fathered, albeit unknowingly, his own destruction, Mordred, who might well be called Merlin's Bane, for he was nothing less than the vengeful implement of the long dead Gorlois. In fact we can begin to see here traces of combat between the Male and Female Principles, and the prize is Britain. As a future poet would sing, 'The older order changeth yielding place to new...'

If Merlin's plan had gone true to form the new order would have been a perfect amalgam of the archetypal Male and Female Principles; instead, because of a mistake, and a feeling of hurt long nurtured into hatred, the whole Great Plan began to show minute but definite cracks.

Arthur, unknowing of the birth of Mordred, continued the plan of uniting the warring factions of Britain. Merlin came and went preparing against the time of Arthur's marriage. Perhaps he still hoped to salvage most of the Plan. An adept of his high rank would not give in easily, if at all; but when the young king met, loved, and wooed the beautiful but shallow Guenevere and declared he would have her and no other as his Queen, Merlin, must have wondered if the gods jested at his expense.

Despite all his arguments Arthur was adamant this was his choice, and who is to say that this whim of a young man, rather than the action of a king, did not also have its cause in the machinations of Morgana/Gorlois and was rooted in revenge? Merlin, in tune with the great Female Power of the Universe, must have known or sensed her barrenness. Certainly he was seer enough to foresee her betrayal, not only of her husband and her marriage vows, but of Arthur's hopes for a united land blessed by the hand of the Mother Goddess whose presence was everywhere proclaimed.

For one who had been dedicated to the Goddess since birth and spent his life serving her this would have been a cruel blow that not even Guenevere's dowry of the Round Table could alleviate. He knew full well that once the marriage took place the chances of founding the dynasty that would meld the old and the new had gone. In effect he had failed in his task. Let us now ask the second question again: 'How is the Great Mother served?' We must answer truthfully and say, 'In tears, in pain, and through the bitter Cup of Sorrows'.

All things concerned with the Great Mother are three wayed so we must expect a third and final question to complete the Triad and the involvement of Merlin as the Priest of the Moon. It is a question that he might well have asked many times as things seemed to fall around him. There would have been other questions pondered over in the dark hours. Had he done all that he could? If he had failed, where had it been? If he could do it all again, would he change anything? Finally in the moments of deepest pain he might have asked of himself, and the Goddess: 'What is to be learned in her Service?'

By now Merlin would have been an old man, perhaps weary of the constant battle to fulfil his appointed task. He might have looked back and tried to judge what might have been saved from the tangle of relationships brought about by the stubbornness and malice of those he had tried to direct according to his knowledge and training in the old ways. During his lifetime those ways had been relegated to the background more and more as the new religion took over the land.

The attempt to graft the new onto the old had failed, but there remained certain tasks that Merlin might bring to birth before he disappeared from the scene. There also remained one obligation that every priest of the Mysteries must fulfil, the training of a successor. Arthur had by now successfully bound the erstwhile small kingdoms into one united land under his own High Kingship. Guenevere, still childless, turned for comfort not to her husband but to his dearest friend and his greatest knight, Lancelot du Lac. Merlin might have had a small human moment and muttered under his breath, 'I told you so.' Perhaps he hoped, vainly as it turned out, that Arthur's bastard son by his half-sister would turn out to be someone he could train for kingship as he had trained Arthur all those years before. This hope was soon dashed when Mordred appeared at court and almost from the first day showed how deeply his character had been warped by his mother. Merlin must have grieved to see him, knowing as he well did, that Morgana had misused the ancient Rite to bring him to birth and in doing so had warped a young mind beyond saving. The Great Mother's Cup of Sorrow must have been bitter indeed for the ageing Priest of the Moon. But there still remained things to be accomplished.

Elaine, who perhaps had always been Merlin's choice to carry the young Priest-King, still lived in her father's castle. She was still the Grail Maiden and as such a more than suitable mother for the Grail Prince. However, a new father must be found; one bastard son was enough for the king to admit to – it would have to be someone else. That someone had to be of high lineage, royal descent, physically perfect and mentally sound. Looking around he could see very few young men who might possibly fulfil the requirements. Gawaine was too warlike, headstrong and hot-tempered. Perceval was dedicated to chastity, Bors already married; it had to be Lancelot. The problem was to win him away from Guenevere, something that Merlin realised would be an impossibility without some form of illusion. Did he heave a sigh when he realised that for the third time a child would have to be conceived through a deception?

First there had been Uther, using the appearance of Gorlois to reach Ygraine and with her under the auspices of the Great Rite bringing Arthur to birth. Then had come the deception of Arthur by Morgana to bring about Mordred, the child of vengeance. Now it would have to be deception again and a third bastard born out of wedlock to achieve the final task, the birth of the Grail Prince. Merlin himself could not be seen to interfere again, more so as the priests of the new religion frowned upon the use of the Great Rite. Now it was time for him to instruct another in the plan and to disappear from the court and indeed from Arthur's life. His work with the High King was done, Arthur must now stand or fall by his own abilities. The time of Merlin had almost passed.

The plan was simple; Lancelot would be deceived by making Elaine look like Guenevere, the same plan that had been used all those long eventful years before and which had been marred by the death of Gorlois. Did the dead man even now reach out across time to demand his price? Might not even Merlin, high Priest of the Moon, Server of the Great Mother-Goddess, hesitate to use the same plan again?

Did the Goddess herself watch over those last preparations and give him the strength to accomplish them. Did she prepare her own great Symbol and superimpose it upon the simple ancient cup that was its physical counterpart? Was it she who manifested the Grail in Arthur's hall that Easter day and inspired the knights to seek it out for themselves? Tired and old, longing for his own peace, Merlin would have set about the task of finding a successor, someone to train and to whom he might pass all the ancient knowledge that was his birthright. It is still traditional for power and position in the mysteries to be passed from man to woman to man and so on. Did this law prevail in those times? Was it because of this that Merlin sought a woman to teach and to use as a go-between to accomplish the last task he might render to Arthur, his foster son? Whatever and wherever, he did seek and he found ... Nimuë, his pupil, his love, and his nemesis.

With the coming of Nimuë the story of Merlin draws to its close. She is destined to be the last of all the women in his life; women that, as at least one tradition would have it, have not touched his heart. Now at the end of his time there comes to him a young and eager girl, full of life, nimble and quick in her understanding, eager to learn and to serve the Priest of the Moon and through him, the Goddess herself.

Legend deals over-harshly with Nimuë, she is dubbed a stealer of wisdom to which she has no right, but are we certain of that? Could it not have been that she was a novice from that ancient school by the Sacred Lake, trained by the high priestess of lost Naradek, now called in our own time the Lady of the Lake? Nimuë could well have been sent by her to aid Merlin in his last days. Certainly there could have been no one better suited to be her teacher, or more gentle in that teaching. Also for the task in hand she was eminently suited to move about the court and between Camelot and the Castle of the Grail without causing any comment – something that would have been impossible for Merlin.

Linked as she is in legend with the water element Nimuë must surely have been the priestess of the Moon for whom Merlin had been lonely through all the weary years. Now she was here, learning, helping and planning the last great task. The court, unlearned in the ways of the ancient faith, may have sniggered behind their hands at the sight of the young maid and the old man, but that would not have worried them. Those who serve the gods need fear no human jibe. Maybe the Goddess herself chose the laughing Nimuë and sent her to the faithful servant to comfort his last days in her service, perhaps to teach him the ultimate lesson, for – remember – we still have to find the answer to the third question.

Even with a new companion to lighten his days Merlin must have despaired at having to resort once more to deception to attain the required end. Did he brood over the long-dead Gorlois, did he with his seership try to reach out and placate the angry shade? I would think not, for he was a man tried by the fires of life, well used to the great Tides of the Inner Levels that sweep across the oceans of time. He would have been used to trimming the sails of his soul to such forces. I am certain he would have bent every last effort in the service of the one to whom he owned his very existence, born to her service and hers alone.

As the plan was perfected the time drew near for Merlin to retreat and to his end they may well have put about certain rumours concerning Nimuë's ambitions. They might have taken care to be seen walking in the sun-dappled woods, her hand in his, her head held to one side as she listened to him speak and teach. Or perhaps beside a stream, his grey head in her lap, she plaiting daisies and meadow flowers into his hair and beard. To the onlookers it would seem to be a case of an 'old man's fancy' turning his head, making a fool of himself in front of the court; but it would not have mattered, only they, and what they were about, mattered now.

We do not know how it happened or when it was, but one day, one bright spring day when the hawthorn was in blossom, Merlin had gone, and only Nimuë was left slipping in and out of the court quietly with a smiling face. Perhaps it was she who lured Lancelot to the castle where Elaine waited to fulfil her part in the plan. They would have been such a contrast, those two maidens, one fair and virginal, of the new faith, the maid of the Grail and soon to be a Grail filled to overflowing herself, the other a priestess of the old ways dedicated to the Great Moon Mother who was offering her ancient Sacred Chalice to be made one with the Christian Cup of Cups. Maybe they sat together in those hours before the arrival of Lancelot, Elaine apprehensive but comforted by the little priestess whose whole life revolved around such rituals.

As the time drew near was it Nimuë who wove the enchantment

that laid the face of Guenevere over that of Elaine and then called the hidden Merlin to walk with her as all those long momentous years before a Priest of the Moon had walked with his mother on her journey to the sacred grove of the Moon? Drawing on his powers, he would have remained unseen until he knew the seed of light that was the promised Grail Child was safe, then, his task done he would have left, maybe to talk awhile with the Guardian of the Grail. They were two priests alike in their power and dedication, one whose tradition and power was on the wane, and one whose star was rising in the east, both knowing the full awesome power that had filled the castle that night.

Before dawn Merlin would have left, setting out on a long last journey back to that place where once he was a young novice. Back to the peace of the College of the Lake, that last bastion of the old ways, there to rest and be refreshed, perhaps, who knows, to come again like Arthur Pendragon. Behind him he left the seed which would one day be Galahad, the Grail Prince. Merlin was content. It would have been a long and arduous journey for an old man, but his heart would have been light, for he must have known that at last he had achieved a part of what he had hoped for in the beginning. The Grail Prince would be born, and though he would not be Arthur's son he would at least be a part of the Round Table; Merlin had made certain that his seat would be ready and waiting. He would not be able to keep the Grail on earth fully manifested, but he would hold it long enough for it to be imprinted upon the race soul. When this was done he would depart with it into the higher realms of existence. He would indeed become the Priest-King, though his kingdom would not be of this earth.

Merlin had failed in his task to make of Britain the land of a blended faith were the old and the new were one on earth, but he had achieved that on a higher level and forever; until the end of time that inner Britain would be a living part of the Old Ways and the Ancient faith of the Sun and the Moon. He had failed to ensure a son for Arthur who would be worthy of his sire, and he knew that Mordred would tear the kingdom apart, but he also knew that something had been sown in those bright years that would live on in the hearts and minds of men and women of the island race. A

legend of legends had been born and the men and women who had
been part of them would be remembered.

When the visions faded and he was still many days' journey away
from his destination, then came the time to ponder the last question
and to seek the answers. For to the third and last question each one
must seek the answer that seems best for them. There is no one right
answer but many that will suffice, and each one who serves must
seek the answer within. Though the old ways fade from surface
memory they remain deep within the ebb and flow of the Racial
Mind. Those who come after are born with it in their blood; though
they may never hear the names of Arthur and Merlin, yet when the
need is there something will rise up in them that cannot be denied
and the old power will flow and grow strong like the waxing moon.

She, the Goddess in whose hands this land has always rested, is
patient and loving. She has worn many faces and borne many names:
Epona and Briganta, Alba and Mona of the Sacred Isle, Arianrhod
and Celemon and Aradia. Her names are a song in the hearts of those
whose bones are made from her soil. Her white horse symbols have
been cut into the chalk hills for untold centuries and the high hills
echo her voice as they did on a day long ago when Merlin climbed
the last hill and looked down on the last refuge of his kind.

They would have come to greet him, perhaps bearing fruit and
wine to ease the last miles, eagerly asking questions of events outside
their quiet valley. He would have noticed how few there were, most
of them old and tired like himself. How glad he must have been to
step inside the cool halls and know there would be no more walking,
no more striving and trying to guide the unguidable. No more court
intrigue and half-heard whispers, just the bird song and the wind in
the trees and the sounds of the deep Lake beyond the door.

They would have let him be for a while to come and go as he
pleased, to adjust to a different set of values, of times and emotions.
He would, I am sure, have spent most of his time in her sanctuary,
easing mind, heart and spirit in her presence. Like the others she
would have waited until he was sure of what he had to say, then
when the time was right she would ask of him: 'Merlin, what have
you learned in my service?'

He would have taken his time, gathering his words like flowers for a garland, each one bright and clear and blending with the whole. He might have quickly thought back to his boyhood when he stood here at his initiation. Then when he was certain he would speak – perhaps it would have been thus: 'My Lady, when I was first brought before you I thought of nothing but your words and your wishes and your commands. I lived only to serve you in all things. I went out into the world at your behest with a plan for that world, thinking myself a priest. I learned humility. First from the people I met upon the road, the poor folk who had little yet shared that little with a stranger. I learned it from the hermit of the new faith who lived alone and shared his bread with the wild things of the forest. I have seen it in a young man raised to kingship weeping the night before his coronation in case he would be a bad king. I have seen it in a knight of purity and courage and seen it blighted in him too. I have seen it in a young maid going to her destiny as the future mother of him who should have been Arthur's son.

'When I had accomplished my first task, I stood here again and I thought of the next task before me. I was proud in your service and secure in my power as a priest. You sent me forth again to accomplish the next part of the plan. Then I learned endurance. I learned that nothing in the physical world can be fully relied upon, I learned that the best of men can set his face against all that is best for him. I learned to keep my faith when all my plans were set at nought. I endured and grew strong. I learned to bend with the forces and not to break but to strive continually, even when it seemed that all was lost.

'For the third time I stood before you and wept that I had failed you so bitterly. My power was set at nought and I was lost. Yet you raised me up and sent me forth again and I went wearily and with an unwilling heart. I learned patience. I learned to wait until the right moment, to bide my time, be it for a Great Rite or for the blooming of a flower. I learned to master time and not take it for my master. Then I learned that from mistakes and failures can come a measure of success unthought of, and I praised you in my heart and finished my task.

'Now I have come before you for almost the last time, and I have pondered on those three things that I have learned, and it seems to me that they are nothing beside the lesson I have learned in the last few days. All these things pass in time but the greatest lesson remains. It cannot be taught to another for each one must learn it for themselves. It is only now, here, in the peace of your sanctuary that I know what I have truly learned in your service. *Great Mother I have learned to understand.'*

The Goddess still watches over these islands. She is still a part of all that makes up the native British Race. Merlin was of the old race of the West, the Drowned Lands, and many of our race share the same blood line. The faith that was new in Merlin's time in its turn has faded, for to everything there is a season of fullness and increase followed by one of waning and decrease, but her symbol, the Great Cup that holds the Ocean of Time, will remain forever.

Short Index of
Works Cited and Quoted

Index